HOW THE EBOOKS WORK

The eBooks are provided in EPUB file format. Please note that you will need an eBook reader installed on your device to open the file. Many devices come with this as standard, but you may still need to install one manually from Google Play.

The eBook content is identical to the content in the printed guide.

HOW TO DOWNLOAD THE WALKING EYE APP

1. Download the Walking Eye App from the App Store or Google Play.
2. Open the app and select the scanning function from the main menu.
3. Scan the QR code on this page – you will then be asked a security question to verify ownership of the book.
4. Once this has been verified, you will see your eBook in the purchased ebook section, where you will be able to download it.

Other destination apps and eBooks are available for purchase separately or are free with the purchase of the Insight Guide book.

INSIGHT ⦿ GUIDES

EXPLORE

LOS ANGELES

⊙ Walking Eye App

YOUR FREE EBOOK AVAILABLE THROUGH THE WALKING EYE APP

Your guide now includes a free eBook to your chosen destination, for the same great price as before. Simply download the Walking Eye App from the App Store or Google Play to access your free eBook.

HOW THE WALKING EYE APP WORKS

Through the Walking Eye App, you can purchase a range of eBooks and destination content. However, when you buy this book, you can download the corresponding eBook for free. Just see below in the grey panel where to find your free content and then scan the QR code at the bottom of this page.

Destinations: Download essential destination content featuring recommended sights and attractions, restaurants, hotels and an A–Z of practical information, all available for purchase.

Ships: Interested in ship reviews? Find independent reviews of river and ocean ships in this section, all available for purchase.

eBooks: You can download your free accompanying digital version of this guide here. You will also find a whole range of other eBooks, all available for purchase.

Free access to travel-related blog articles about different destinations, updated on a daily basis.

CONTENTS

ART LOVERS

Artistic highlights include the Getty Center (route 12), Los Angeles County Museum of Art (route 7), and The Broad (route 1). Fans of ancient Greece and Rome should check out the Getty Villa (route 13).

RECOMMENDED ROUTES FOR...

CHILDREN

Step into storybook worlds at Disneyland (route 6) and visit all your movie favorites at Universal Studios (route 5). Learn while playing at the California Science Center (route 10), or just enjoy a day at Venice Beach or Santa Monica Pier (both route 3).

FOODIES

Munch your way around Asia in Chinatown (route 8), Little Tokyo (route 9) and Koreatown (route 7). Visit some of the city's best restaurants in Hollywood (route 3), Beverly Hills (route 4) and West Hollywood (route 13).

HISTORY BUFFS

Los Angeles was founded by Spanish and Mexican colonists at El Pueblo (route 8), while the movie industry got started in Hollywood in the early 20th century (route 2). Natural history and African American history are on show at Exposition Park (route 10).

NATURE LOVERS

Go whale-watching off Long Beach (route 15), stroll the strands of Will Rogers State Beach (route 3), or hike the rolling hills of Griffith Park (route 11). For a view to remember, Mulholland Drive takes you high above the city (route 12).

NIGHT OWLS

Grab a drink at historic Musso & Frank Grill and trawl Hollywood Boulevard at night (route 2), take in a live band at Sunset Strip venues like Whisky-a-Go-Go (route 13), or sample the student nightlife in Westwood (route 14).

SHOPPING

Peruse the posh boutiques of Rodeo Drive (route 4), the hip stores along Melrose Avenue (route 13), and the markets of Chinatown (route 8). Santa Monica (route 3) and Westwood (route 14) are also happy hunting grounds for shopaholics.

TOP ARCHITECTURE

Downtown Los Angeles (route 1) features everything from soaring skyscrapers to Art Deco gems like LA Library. Both USC (route 10) and UCLA campuses (route 14) are crammed with stately, historic buildings.

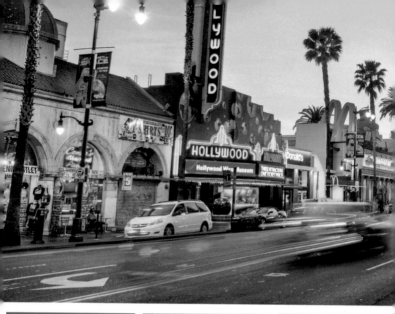

INTRODUCTION

An introduction to Los Angeles's geography, customs and culture, plus illuminating background information on cuisine, history, and what to do when you're there.

EXPLORE LOS ANGELES

The City of Angels, Tinseltown, or just 'La–La Land,' Los Angeles is known the world over for year–round sunshine and palm trees, the movies of Hollywood, the glamor of Beverly Hills, and golden surf beaches.

Los Angeles is a relatively young city, and despite its Hispanic roots, is inexorably linked to modern pop culture and a health-conscious, laid-back 'SoCal' lifestyle. The city inspired California's modern surfing boom in the 1950s, the music of the Beach Boys and the Doors in the 1960s, the skateboarders of 1970s Dogtown, and the West Coast hip-hop scene in the late 1980s. Today, it's home to world-class art museums, Universal Studios, Disneyland, the Sunset Strip, and major sports franchises the Lakers and the Dodgers.

GEOGRAPHY AND LAYOUT

Los Angeles is truly vast, a fact hard to absorb until you actually get here. LA is only America's second biggest city in terms of population, but it's stitched together by an intricate network of freeways crossing 1,000 sq miles (2,590 sq km). The core of the city lies in a flat, arid basin between the Pacific Ocean and the Santa Monica and San Gabriel mountains, but it's some 15 miles (24km) between Downtown and the coast. Major suburban communities lie across the mountains in the San Fernando and San Gabriel valleys, while Malibu lies farther west along the coast. Long Beach, Pasadena, Burbank, and Anaheim are all independently administered cities, but fall squarely within LA's metropolitan sprawl.

The tours in this book begin with the key areas of interest – Downtown, Hollywood, and so on – then proceed geographically across the city. Most can be completed on foot, or with minimal use of public transportation, though some (Mulholland Drive, for example) require a car.

Contrary to popular belief, LA does have efficient public transportation, with Metro lines and buses now providing the best method of zipping around the city without your own wheels.

Traditionally, the most popular way to get around LA has been to drive; with nearly two vehicles per household, LA is one of the world's highest per-capita car populations. However, traffic is bumper-to-bumper much of the day (it's often described as 'stop-and-start' by local media). Taxis are

Surfin' USA

widely available but fairly expensive for long distances, and you'll often have to call them by phone (or use Uber).

HISTORY

The Los Angeles region was settled by Chumash and Tongva peoples thousands of years before the arrival of Spanish settlers on September 4, 1781 (a date commemorated by the LA County Fair each year). The settlers named it Los Angeles after the Spanish phrase for 'Our Lady Queen of the Angels' (ie Mary, the mother of

LA traffic

Jesus). In 1821, a still tiny Los Angeles became part of newly independent Mexico. Even after being swallowed up by the US after the Mexican–American War in 1846, Los Angeles remained largely insignificant, a small town of less than 5,000, comprising white American immigrants, poor Chinese laborers, and wealthy Mexican ranchers. The arrival of the transcontinental railroad gave the city a massive boost in 1876, and LA's population exploded – by 1920 it was over half a million.

By 1912, movie companies such as Paramount, Warner Bros, RKO, and Columbia were setting up production in LA, and by the 1920s Hollywood was entering its golden age. In 1932, Los Angeles hosted the Summer Olympics, confirming its arrival on the world stage (Los Angeles hosted the Olympics again in 1984, and will host the Games for a third time in 2028). More boom years followed World War II – LA eclipsed Chicago as the nation's second-largest metropolis in 1980. But as workers flocked to LA to find jobs, overcrowding, prejudice, and social ranking would continue to cause great tensions. Racial unrest has come to a head more than once here: in 1965, the Watts Riots lasted six days and left 32 dead, while the riots of 1992, a reaction to the arrest and beating of Rodney King by the LAPD, resulted in a death toll of 63. Crime has since tailed off from its

Skateboarding has been popular in LA since the 1970s

1990s highs, reaching a 50-year low in 2013. Democrat Antonio Villaraigosa became the city's first elected Latino mayor in 2005.

Today, LA seems to be re-inventing itself yet again, as indie musicians, writers, and designers (many fleeing high rents in San Francisco) are colonizing neighborhoods such as Echo Park, Highland Park, and Silver Lake, adding a Bohemian and artistic vibe to a city often stereotyped as being in thrall to the glitz and glamor of celebrity.

CLIMATE

Los Angeles has a warm, Mediterranean climate, with low annual rainfall and full days of sunshine between May and October – though LA's notorious smog is at its worst when temperatures are highest, in August and September. In the winter it can get chilly at night, and you'll need a light jacket. Note that temperatures in the San Fernando and San Gabriel valleys are considerably warmer, while the deserts beyond are boiling hot in the summer. Spring and fall are the best times to visit, while summers can be extremely busy.

POPULATION

Greater Los Angeles is one of the most populous areas in the world, with around 19 million inhabitants. Immigration from Asia and Mexico continues to boost numbers (LA is now over 50 percent Latino, with Spanish spoken as much as English as a first language). The city itself has a population of around 4 million (2016 estimate), with sizeable African-American (10 percent) and Asian (15 percent) communities.

Few places on earth attract such a diverse population. In all, the city is home to people from over 140 countries speaking 224 different languages. Mexican ancestry makes up the largest Latino group, though Salvadoran and Guatemalan commu-

Downtown LA

Star-spotting on the Hollywood Walk of Fame

nities are growing. Cultural enclaves like Chinatown, Historic Filipinotown, Koreatown, Little Armenia, Little Ethi- opia, Tehrangeles, Little Tokyo, Lit- tle Bangladesh, and Thai Town have added to the city's tourist appeal.

DON'T LEAVE LA WITHOUT...

Sipping cocktails at Musso & Frank Grill. This classically dark and moody watering hole has long been a favorite hangout for movie stars of the Golden Age and today's brattier celebrities. See page 43.

Taking in the scene at Venice Beach. Trawling the promenade between Santa Monica and Venice is an LA tradition, taking in the surfers, sand, muscle-men, skaters, and assorted eccentrics. See page 44.

Soaking up art at The Getty Center. A colossal, Modernist arts center, the Getty is stuffed with treasures of the Old World. Its hillside setting provides great views of the metropolis. See page 89.

Traversing Mulholland Drive by car. This scenic route runs along the crest of the Hollywood Hills, providing magnif- icent vistas of the Los Angeles basin and the San Fernando Valley. It is especially beautiful at night, when the lights of the city shimmer below. See page 87.

Sampling the French-dip sandwiches at Philippe the Original. This 1908 sawdust café serves up its eponymous sandwich with turkey, ham, lamb, pork, or beef dipped in roasting-pan juices. See page 74.

Munching an old-fashioned at Ran- dy's Donuts. This 1950s Pop Art fixture is hard to miss, thanks to the colossal doughnut on its roof. Open 24/7, you can sate your sweet tooth any time of the day or night. See page 121.

Enjoying the traditional Mexican vibe at El Pueblo. The original historic dis- trict of Los Angeles has an authentic Spanish-style feel and features muse- ums, stores, and Mexican restaurants. Many events are held here, from a week- end-long celebration of Cinco de Mayo in May to the Los Angeles birthday celebra- tion in August and Mexican Independ- ence Day in September. See page 95.

Admiring the fabulous contemporary art at The Broad. LA's newest art gallery is one of the best in America, a futuris- tic space containing Pop Art icons galore. See page 35.

Perusing the stars on the Hollywood Walk of Fame. Follow the famous pink terrazzo and brass stars embedded in the sidewalks along 15 blocks of Hol- lywood Boulevard. Among the most sought-after are those of Marilyn Mon- roe, Charlie Chaplin, and John Wayne. See page 41.

Taking a studio tour. Get behind the scenes at Paramount, Universal, and Warner Bros, who all offer illuminat- ing tours of their LA studios. See pages 43 and 56.

LOCAL CUSTOMS

Being such a cosmopolitan, multi-cultural city, Los Angeles is home to a wide variety of peoples, customs, and traditions, though a relaxed 'SoCal' (Southern Californian) lifestyle – revolving around the beach, the gym, and healthy eating – is certainly prominent. Having said that, life for many Angelenos still centers on the car and the daily headaches associated with bumper-to-bumper traffic – arguing about the fastest route between two locations in the city is a favorite LA pastime. Many museums close on Mondays and/or Tuesdays, though stores and services tend to operate all week long, even during public holidays.

POLITICS AND ECONOMICS

Los Angeles is governed by an elected city council and a mayor (elected to four-year terms, serving no more than two terms). Democrat Eric Garcetti was voted in as mayor in 2013 (winning again in 2017), becoming the city's first Jewish leader. The city is generally left-leaning and tends to vote Democrat, like much of California: Hilary Clinton received over 70 percent of the vote here in the 2016 presidential election.

LA is the third-largest economic metropolitan area in the world, after Tokyo and New York, driven by international trade and entertainment (TV, movies, video games, and music recording), but also aerospace, technology, petroleum, fashion, and tourism. The port of LA and Long Beach handles more than 60 percent of the ocean-going cargo coming to the West Coast. Paramount Pictures, 21st Century Fox, Sony, Warner Bros, Universal Pictures, and Walt Disney Studios are all based here, while SpaceX (owned by Elon Musk), Snapchat, Trader Joe's, Princess Cruise Lines, Hulu, and Dole Food Co all call LA home.

These days Los Angeles is safer than it's been in decades, with public transportation better than ever, a host of new attractions, and the most diverse culinary scene in the nation – it's a great time to visit.

Paramount Pictures presents...

The panoramic view from the Griffith Observatory

TOP TIPS FOR VISITING LA

Reserve The Broad. It's crucial to make reservations for special exhibitions at The Broad, as your ticket will also allow timed entry to the permanent galleries (and skip the long lines). Reserve tickets online at https://ticketing.thebroad.org.

Buy a travel pass. For longer stays in LA, buy a seven-day MTA pass for $25, valid on the Metro and on city buses.

See the Sign. The best views of the famous Hollywood Sign can be had from the Griffith Park Observatory – you can hike to the sign itself, but the path only runs above it (it's strictly forbidden to get any closer).

Free museums. USC's Fisher Museum of Art, plus the nearby California Science Center, and California African American Museum, in Exposition Park, offer free admission. The world-class Getty Center is also free.

Drivers – avoid I-405. This is the worst highway in LA, and can get gridlocked at any time.

Beach essentials. LA's beaches are gorgeous, but remember that the water is cold, even in summer. The sun, however, is extremely strong, even in winter; always use UV protection when outdoors. You can get burned even if it's overcast or there's a cool breeze, so don't take a chance.

Seeing the stars. To see which 'star' is being unveiled on Hollywood Boulevard on any given week, visit www.walkoffame. com/pages/upcoming-ceremonies; ceremonies are free to attend.

Attend the Oscars red carpet. The annual Academy Awards (usually early March) is a star-studded, strictly invitation-only affair, but anyone can apply for a seat at the red carpet (the long media corridor where the stars parade before entering the Dolby Theatre in Hollywood). Apply for the 'Oscars Red Carpet Fan Experience' at www.oscars.org in the fall, which is essentially a lottery – the lucky 1,000 winners get free seats on the red carpet bleachers.

Escape the crowds. Avoiding the crowds at many of the attractions in Los Angeles, is, in essence, down to timing. Theme parks will obviously not be as busy during school time as they will be during vacation time, and in general, most places won't be as busy during the week as they would be on weekends or even public holidays.

Don't forget to tip. Waiters earn most of their income from tips, and not leaving a fair amount is seen as an insult. Wait staff expect tips of at least 15 percent, and up to 20 percent for very good service. When sitting at a bar, you should leave at least a dollar per round for the barkeeper; more if the round is more than two drinks.

Take out insurance. Health care, especially hospitalization, is extremely expensive in the United States. Some hospitals might even refuse treatment without proof of insurance. Overseas visitors should therefore make arrangements before leaving home for health insurance with a high level of coverage.

Modern Californian cuisine

FOOD AND DRINK

Given its glamorous associations, it's no surprise that LA is one of America's culinary hotspots. From gourmet restaurants to authentic Korean canteens and Mexican tacquerías, Los Angeles offers an incredible range of dining experiences.

Mexican food is the closest thing to an indigenous LA cuisine, while purveyors of East Asian food and gourmet street carts have also flourished in recent years. Many of the city's higher-end restaurants serve contemporary California cuisine, the signature style of top-notch LA eating, blending French-style food with fresh local ingredients in an eclectic, harmonious brew.

LOCAL CUISINE

Given its multicultural make-up, LA's outlook on cuisine is international. While all-American burgers and fries are certainly easy to find, authentic foods from every corner of the world are far more prominent, from Cuba to Armenia, Ethiopia to Brazil. Some trends do stand out however, beginning with a love of everything Mexican.

South of the border (Mexican)
With Tijuana just a three-hour drive away, it's no surprise that Mexican cuisine has flourished in LA. East LA is the Hispanic heart of the city and the best place to find authentic eateries. Taco and burrito joints predominate, mostly simple hole-in-the-walls and food trucks (like Al & Bea's Mexican Food, or Cactus Taqueria, see page 114). There's much more to Mexican cuisine than this, however, with contemporary dishes served at restaurants such as Broken Spanish (www.brokenspanish.com), Oaxacan mole showcased at Guelaguetza (www.ilovemole.com) and Tlayuda (www.tlayudala.com), and Yucatecán specialties offered at Chichen Itza (www.chichenitzarestaurant.com). Toca Madera West Hollywood (www.tocamadera.com) is the place for upscale, gourmet Mexican dining.

Modern Californian
Californian cooking is essentially fusion cuisine, using fresh, locally produced, seasonal ingredients. Though the modern Californian food movement is more closely associated with the San Francisco area, Wolfgang Puck was also an early pioneer (especially with the popularization of themed 'California-style' pizza at Spago, see page 55). Today, LA features several high-end purveyors of food-to-table Californian cuisine, from Redbird (see page 113) to Otium (see page 113) and Water Grill (see page 114).

A chilled margarita

Go east (Asian)

Los Angeles is an international city, but thanks to a large immigrant population, it does East Asian food especially well. The Chinese, Filipinos, Japanese, Koreans, and Thais all have their own enclaves bursting with restaurants, while the Vietnamese are also well represented. Sugarfish (see page 113), Mr Chow (see page 117), Soowon Galbi Korean BBQ (see page 118), Daikokuya (see page 119), and Sanamluang Café (see page 119) are great examples.

WHERE TO EAT

You'll find places to eat spread throughout LA's numerous neighborhoods, though there are some especially good areas for restaurants. The options Downtown have improved in recent years, especially in the Arts District. Cultural enclaves such as Little Tokyo and Chinatown, Koreatown, Thai Town, Historic Filipinotown, and Little Ethiopia offer authentic eating experiences, while hipster joints thrive in Echo Park and Silver Lake. Hollywood (and West Hollywood), Melrose, Santa Monica, and Venice remain top places for restaurants and nightlife, while Beverly Hills boasts high-end bistros and Westwood contains cheaper, student-oriented spots.

Chain restaurants

All the usual fast-food suspects are here, but there are some native Californian and Angeleno names worth seeking out. King of California's fast-food burger scene is In-N-Out Burger, founded in the San Gabriel Valley in 1948. Today there are branches all over the city selling its signature cheeseburgers and 'double-doubles.' Rival Umami Burger debuted in 2009. Pinkberry, the frozen yogurt franchise, was founded in West Hollywood in 2005. Though the buzz has died down somewhat, its silky smooth products still have a cult following. Health-conscious Tender Greens first opened in 2006, with 17 branches and counting in the LA area today, serving organic salads and sandwiches. Mexican food specialist Loteria Grill is a relative newcomer, while 800 Degrees Wood-Fired Kitchen has built up a local pizza empire. Chef Kazunori Nozawa's cult sushi restaurant Sugarfish has blossomed into a chain since its 2008 debut, as has Lemonade (which opened in the same year, serving pre-made salads, pot roasts, and various flavors of

---

Healthy eating, LA style

In the movie *LA Story* (1991), Steve Martin's character famously orders a 'half double decaffeinated half-caf, with a twist of lemon,' and Angelenos have retained a reputation for being spectacularly particular when it comes to food and drink (Martin was joking, but today you really can order a 'doppio macchiato half-caf skim foam'). It's a city where bread is considered unhealthy, and eating organic, gluten-free, and vegan is second nature.

Yellowtail sashimi with jalapeño at Nobu

lemonade). Other local chains include Mendocino Farms, serving sandwiches made with fresh organic, vegan, and vegetarian ingredients, and Zankou Chicken, a family-owned chain of Lebanese *shawarma* and rotisserie chicken outlets.

Celebrity chefs

With dozens of upscale restaurants spread all over the city, diners will find plenty of choices for a memorable meal in Los Angeles. Several are overseen by internationally acclaimed or celebrity chefs. Among the biggies represented here are Wolfgang Puck, who runs several establishments, notably Spago in Beverly Hills (see page 55); sushi master Nobu Matsuhisa (see page 117); Mexican specialist Rick Bayless (Red O); and Niki Nakayama, whose N/Naka Restaurant specializes in modern Japanese *kaiseki* cuisine. Australian celebrity chef Curtis Stone opened Maude in Beverly Hills in 2014, while TV's *Top Chef* winner Michael Voltaggio runs ink and ink.sack, both in West Hollywood. Even movie stars have got in on the action: Ryan Gosling has Tagine in Beverly Hills, while Robert De Niro is behind Tuscan gem Ago in West Hollywood. Small plates innovator José Andrés founded Tres by José Andrés, while TV chef Scott Conant runs The Ponte, a contemporary Italian restaurant in West Hollywood.

Diners

In a city so associated with the automobile, the classic American diner has a special place in Los Angeles. Many of the oldest restaurants here are diners, retaining 1950s counters and booths, and often cooking up bargain plates of eggs, bacon, and waffles for breakfast, and chops and steaks for dinner. Downtown, Clifton's Cafeteria (since 1935; see page 112) was a favorite of Ray Bradbury, while Cole's Pacific Electric Buffet (see page 113) was founded way back in 1908 – ancient by LA standards.

Some joints specialize in specific dishes. Philippe the Original French Dip (see page 74) serves meat sandwiches dipped in roasting-pan juices, while the signatures at Original Tommy's Hamburgers, and Roscoe's House of Chicken and Waffles (see page 115), are self-explanatory.

The 'googie' diner emerged in the 1960s, with its futuristic architecture influenced by the Space Age hopes of the era. Fabulous examples in LA include Mel's Drive-in (see page 59) and Pann's (see page 121).

Food trucks

LA's food truck scene is extremely diverse, with everything from simple tacos and kebabs to gourmet hotdogs and Korean food on offer. Always check websites or Twitter for the latest locations and times. Solid options include Indian food specialist Bollywood Bites, Guerrilla Tacos, and the lobster rolls at Lobsta Truck. Ricky's Fish Tacos serves highly sought after Ensenada-style catfish and shrimp tacos.

Fish tacos　　　　　　　　　　　　　　　*A creative latte*

DRINKS

Los Angeles has all sorts of interesting places to raise a glass of your favorite tipple, from classy hotel lounges to historic dive bars, raucous sports bars, and dazzling nightclubs. A number of bars have Happy Hour specials on cocktails and bottled beers. Always take photo identification that gives your birthdate if you want to enjoy an alcoholic drink: you must be 21 years old, and able to prove it.

Beer

Los Angeles has not been immune to the huge explosion of craft or micro-brewed beers in the US over the last few decades, though most top Californian names hail from the northern part of the state. The heart of the scene is Downtown, where you should seek out Arts District Brewing Co (www.213hospitality.com/artsdistrictbrewing), Bonaventure Brewing Co (BBC; www.bonaventurebrewing.com), or Boomtown Brewery (https://boomtownbrew.com), among others. In Venice, try Firestone Walker Brewing (www.firestonebeer.com).

Wine and cocktails

Though very little wine is produced in LA itself, the city lies close to several world-class grape-producing regions (notably Napa and Sonoma), and its bars and supermarkets are liberally stocked with fine vintages. In the city, seek out San Antonio Winery (https://sanantoniowinery.com), Moraga Estate (www.moragablair.com), or Cobblestone Vineyards (www.cobblestonewine.com). In Malibu, there's Rosenthal Winery (https://rosenthalestatewines.com) and Malibu Wines (www.malibuwines.com). Though drinking in LA wine bars and lounges is rarely cheap, the quality is very good, with all the top names from around the world readily available. When it comes to craft cocktails, the city is in a class of its own, with 'mixologists' competing on not just martinis, mojitos, and pina coladas, but on a host of weird and wacky concoctions made with everything from garden herbs to exotic fruits. The Dresden Room (see page 122), Tiki Ti (see page 123), Walker Inn (see page 123), and The Varnish (see page 124) are good bets.

Coffee and tea

Los Angeles is a very coffee-savvy city. Here, even hotel breakfast buffets offer quality brands in different strengths to suit everyone's tastes. Super-serious local coffee shops include G&B Coffee in Grand Central Market (see page 37), and Urth Caffé (see page 121), which also sells fine teas. Portland's Stumptown, Chicago's Intelligentsia (see page 114), Oakland's beloved Blue Bottle, and Santa Cruz-based Verve Coffee Roasters are also well-represented.

You can get hot tea at most cafés and restaurants, and green and herbal teas are widely available. Iced tea is an American favorite and, like filter coffee, often comes with free refills. It's often served already sweetened.

Rodeo Drive mannequin

SHOPPING

Shopping in LA is an art – besides the run-of-the-mill chain retailers there are big department stores and mega-sized malls where most of the hardcore shopping goes on, and of course Rodeo Drive, two blocks of the world's most exclusive boutiques.

If there was ever a shopping heaven, this is it. Everything you could possibly want is at your disposal with a flash of the credit card. With hundreds of stores located along charming streets, stacked in mega-malls, and tucked into nondescript neighborhood nooks, there's no doubt you'll find more than a few mementos to carry home.

SHOPPING AREAS

Rodeo Drive and Melrose Avenue are LA's twin centers of high fashion, both thoroughfares crammed with boutiques. Note also that ethnic enclaves such as Chinatown (see page 73), Koreatown (see page 68), and Little Tokyo (see page 75) are packed with markets and malls selling souvenirs, exotic foods, cheap clothes, and toys. Old Town Pasadena is also a pleasant place to browse.

Rodeo Drive (Beverly Hills)
The first stop on every shopper's circuit is Rodeo Drive (www.rodeodrive-bh. com). This is where leading designers showcase their fashions to a rich, glamorous, and sophisticated clientele, the likes of Gucci, Hermès, Armani, and Tiffany, but more affordable retailers such as Ralph Lauren and Guess vie for tourist dollars (see page 50 for more on Rodeo Drive).

Melrose Avenue
Funky and youthful attire is offered at every doorstep along Melrose Avenue (see page 90), between La Brea and Fairfax. Once the epicenter of hip Hollywood counterculture, this strip has become a strolling street for young tourists. Still, there are plenty of bargains to be found.

Melrose Avenue carries on into West Hollywood, where, amid the art galleries and design showrooms, you'll find exorbitantly expensive Fred Segal, the best and most celebrity-frequented mini-department store in town. Another favorite is elite clothing store Maxfield (www. maxfieldla.com), which carries a range of top designers.

Beverly Grove and Fairfax District
Beverly Grove, south of West Hollywood, is the Melrose alternative, especially along Third Street between La Cienega and Fairfax, with a hipper and

Enjoying a shopping spree in Santa Monica

more stylish feel, along with antiques, clothing, shoe, and gift stores. Robertson Boulevard (between Beverly Boulevard and Third Street; www.robertsonboulevard-shop.com) is the best place to spot celebs as they dash into trendy boutiques like Rebecca Taylor and Lauren Moshi. Meanwhile, La Brea Avenue (the blocks between Wilshire and Melrose) and Beverly Boulevard (between La Brea and Stanley) are for the stylish locals too old for Melrose fashion and too hip for Rodeo. Along both streets are retro furnishings, vintage clothing, designer boutiques, and fun gift shops.

Santa Monica and Venice
In Santa Monica, hip Main Street celebrates everything from thrift shops to chic boutiques, while Montana Avenue is known for pricey upscale designer apparel and furnishings. The eternally crowded Third Street Promenade (a three-block pedestrian mall) caters to both tourist and local markets with an enormous choice of affordable chain clothing stores, street performers, jewelry shops, and gift boutiques.

In Venice, Abbot Kenny Boulevard features fashionable stores such as Burro (https://burrogoods.com) and Heist (www.shopheist.com).

Los Feliz
The few blocks of Vermont Avenue above Prospect Avenue in laid-back hipster neighborhood Los Feliz are home to some of the underground's groovier stores; Co-op 28 (www.coop28.com), Half Off Clothing Store (https://halfoffclothingstore.com), Otherwild (https://otherwild.com), Skylight Books (www.skylightbooks.com), and Leap at 1756 N. Vermont Avenue among them.

Over on Hillhurst Avenue you'll find unusual gifts at Spitfire Girl (www.spitfiregirl.com), and designer Carol Young (www.carolyoung.com).

Silver Lake
Silver Lake is another hipster 'hood known for its vintage stores, indie coffee shops, home goods, records, and fashion boutiques. Highlights include the high-end clothing, shoes, accessories and homewares at Mohawk

The Piñata District

Downtown LA is laced with wholesale shopping districts, offering everything from flowers and toys to fabrics and sewing machines. The most intriguing to explore is the Piñata District at Olympic Boulevard and Central Avenue (extending between 8th and 10th streets), where, surprise, surprise, the main product is multicolored Mexican piñatas in all shapes and sizes – stores here carry all the kitschy toys and treats to put in your piñata, too. There are boxes of spicy Mexican sweets, dried chilies, and, on weekends, street vendors selling all manner of tasty snacks.

Vendor at Santa Monica's vibrant farmers' market

General Store (www.mohawkgeneralstore.com), trendy Lacausa Clothing (www.lacausaclothing.com), and French-born designer Clare Vivier (www.clarev.com).

Fashion District (Downtown LA)

LA's Fashion District (www.fashiondistrict.org) is the hub of the West Coast garment industry. It covers 90 blocks southeast of central Downtown, spreading out from a hub around Los Angeles and 11th streets. Most of the designer showrooms are wholesale businesses, but there are also hundreds of retail stores that sell discounted clothing and accessories. On Saturdays many wholesale-only stores sell to the general public.

The Jewelry District is also located on nearby Hill Street, between West 5th and West 6th streets, while the Santee Alley flea market (www.thesanteealley.com) is located between Santee Street, Maple Avenue, Olympic Boulevard, and 12th Street.

MALLS AND SHOPPING CENTERS

In a town where time in traffic is to be avoided at all costs, one-stop shopping is essential. In shopping malls, everything you're looking for is available without moving your car. The Beverly Hills set usually bops over to Westfield Century City (www.westfield.com/centurycity), a pleasant open-air mall with a stadium-seating movie theater. Bordering West Hollywood and Beverly Hills is the 200-plus store Beverly Center (www.beverlycenter.com); Westwood has the Westside Pavilion (www.westsidepavilion.com); while in the Fairfax District the Farmers' Market has expanded into The Grove (https://thegrovela.com), a smart outdoor shopping area with upscale chain stores.

By the sea, head for Santa Monica Place mall (www.santamonicaplace.com) at the end of the Third Street Promenade. The Hollywood & Highland shopping and entertainment complex (see page 38) anchors Hollywood Boulevard's main entertainment district, while CityWalk (100 Universal City Plaza, Universal City; www.citywalkhollywood.com) has a wide range of retail wonders, including magic shops, toy stores, and science-fiction memorabilia (see page 59).

Department stores such as Macy's, Nordstrom, Bloomingdale's, Neiman-Marcus, Saks Fifth Avenue, and Barneys New York (the latter three with valet parking) are strategically located around town, often in more than one location. Many can be found along Wilshire Boulevard in Beverly Hills.

OUTDOOR MARKETS

Strolling the city's open-air markets is an excellent way to grab some delicious and inexpensive grub and mingle with the locals.

Amoeba Music

The famous Farmers' Market at Third and Fairfax is a mixture of old folks, tourists, and hip Hollywood types who crowd the excellent food stands. Santa Monica's outdoor farmers' market is held Wednesday and Saturday 8.30am–1pm along Arizona Avenue at the Third Street Promenade.

Smaller farmers' markets are held on every day of the week in different locations throughout the city. Downtown's Grand Central Market on Broadway is LA's oldest and largest open-air produce market (see page 37). Also Downtown is the Flower Market, on Wall and 8th streets; the best selections are found before dawn.

BOOKS

The city has more than a dozen specialty bookstores, including Skylight Books (see above); the Bodhi Tree on Melrose (www.bodhitree.com), which carries metaphysical and New Age titles; and Book Soup on Sunset Boulevard (www.booksoup.com), which also carries international newspapers and periodicals. The Last Bookstore (453 S. Spring Street) in Downtown LA is a vast emporium of used and new books, while Hennessey + Ingalls (300 S. Santa Fe Avenue) specializes in art, architecture, and design, and Kinokuniya Los Angeles in Little Tokyo's Weller Court Shopping Center is a one-stop shop for Asian books and comics. Children's Book World (10580 W. Pico Boulevard) offers reading materials for kids of all ages. Meltdown Comics (7522 Sunset Boulevard) features comic books, graphic novels, manga, toys, and collectibles.

MUSIC STORES

LA's music capital status is backed up by numerous record stores that still exist here, even in the age of iTunes and Spotify.

The most famous is Amoeba Music (6400 W. Sunset Boulevard, Hollywood; www.amoeba.com), boasting a vast selection of titles – supposedly numbering around half a million – on CD, tape, and vinyl, which you can listen to at booths throughout the store. Nearby, The Record Parlour (6408 Selma Avenue; www.therecordparlour.com) offers a similar experience.

Over in Silver Lake, Rockaway Records (2395 Glendale Boulevard; www.rockaway.com) sells both used CDs and LPs, as well as DVDs. Record Surplus in Santa Monica (12436 Santa Monica Boulevard; www.record surplusla.com) contains a massive LP collection of surf music, ancient rock'n'roll, 1960s soundtracks, and unintentionally hilarious spoken-word recordings. Fingerprints Music in Long Beach (420 E. 4th Street; http://finger printsmusic.com) is another indie outfit, offering alternative-leaning CD and vinyl, plus in-store performances from local rockers.

Scott Weiland takes center stage at The Viper Room

ENTERTAINMENT

As the entertainment capital of the world, Los Angeles offers everything from multicultural theater, classical music, and ballet, to world-famous comedy clubs, rock venues, glamorous nightclubs, and live tapings of America's favorite TV shows.

Nightlife in LA is among the best in the country, with many options for serious partying and debauchery. The city also has an overwhelming choice of high-caliber live music, performing arts, and comedy. Not surprisingly, though, film is still the chief cultural staple of the region.

NIGHTLIFE

The clubs of LA range from posh velvet-rope hangouts to industrial noise cellars. Many of the hottest club nights are transient, especially those catering to the house, ambient, techno, or hip-hop scenes; always check LA Weekly (www.laweekly.com) or Time Out (www.timeout.com/los-angeles) before setting out. Most of the top clubs are either in Hollywood or West Hollywood, while Downtown is home to a handful of itinerant clubs operating above and below board. LA also has an established LGBTQ scene.

Weekend nights are the busiest, but during the week things are often cheaper. Where they exist, cover charges range widely (often $5–20). Except at all-ages, alcohol-free clubs, the minimum age is 21 – bring ID.

LIVE MUSIC

Since the nihilistic punk bands of 30 years ago distanced the city from its spaced-out cocaine-cowboy image, LA's rock and pop scene has been second to none. The home of Guns N' Roses, Metallica, Red Hot Chili Peppers, Green Day, and Linkin Park (named after Santa Monica's Lincoln Park) has been revitalized by artists and bands such as Banks, Haim, Hollywood Undead, Local Natives, and Shlohmo.

As the cradle of West Coast gangster rap, hip-hop is also prevalent, whether mixed in dance music by Westside DJs or in its more authentic form in the inner city (best avoided by out-of-towners). Legendary rock venues such as The Roxy, The Viper Room, and Whisky-a-Go-Go (see page 90) are still going strong. LA also has a small but vibrant country and folk scene, found at places such as Kulak's Woodshed (www.kulakswoodshed.com), while Rusty's Surf Ranch in Santa Monica is the spot for classic surf music (www.rustyssurfranch.com).

Most venues open at 8 or 9pm; headline bands are usually onstage between 11pm and 1am. Cover (or ticket) prices range widely from $5 to $75.

Los Angeles Philharmonic's Walt Disney Concert Hall

CLASSICAL MUSIC AND DANCE

The Los Angeles Philharmonic (Disney Hall) and LA Opera (The Music Center) are the major names for classical music and opera in the city, and perform regularly in their respective venues in Downtown LA. Contemporary dance and ballet is also well represented, with the Los Angeles Ballet (https://losangelesballet.org) usually featuring a November–May program with standards like the *Nutcracker* and a good number of new and modern works.

THEATER

While the bigger venues host a predictable array of musicals and classics with an all-star cast, more than a hundred small theaters can be found around LA. A big show will set you back at least $50, with smaller shows around $10–20.

Major theaters include the Actors' Gang in Culver City (www.theactorsgang.com), where actor Tim Robbins is Artistic Director, the Ahmanson Theatre (www.centertheatregroup.org) Downtown, and the Geffen Playhouse in Westwood (www.geffenplayhouse). For Fringe productions, check out The Complex in Hollywood (www.complexhollywood.com), a group of alternative companies revolving around five small theaters, and Hudson Theatres in Hollywood (www.hudsontheatre.com). Other indie outfits include Open Fist Theatre (www.openfist.org) and the Theatricum Botanicum (www.theatricum.com) in the Santa Monica Mountains, presenting a range of classic and modern plays in an idyllic outdoor setting.

COMEDY

LA has a wide range of comedy clubs. While rising stars can be spotted on the underground open-mike scene, most of the famous comics appear at the more established clubs in Hollywood, West LA, or the valleys. These venues usually put on two shows per evening – the later one being more popular. Notable venues include the Comedy & Magic Club (www.comedyandmagicclub.com) where Jay Leno tests material, the Comedy Store (see page 125), Groundlings (see page 125), The Improv (https://improv.com), the Laugh Factory (www.laughfactory.com), and Second City Studio Theater (www.secondcity.com).

La La jazz

Fans of the movie *La La Land* will be pleased to know that jazz is alive and well in LA. West Coast jazz developed in Los Angeles and San Francisco during the 1950s; Central Avenue was once the city's jazz hub, commemorated by the annual Central Avenue Jazz Festival (last weekend in July). Today, venues such as the Baked Potato (www.thebakedpotato.com), Grand Star Jazz Club (www.grandstarjazz-club.com), and The Mint (www.themintla.com) all host a decent roster of local and international talent.

Pasadena's Rose Bowl stadium

ACTIVITIES

LA has a justified reputation as one of America's sports capitals, with iconic teams such as the Lakers, Dodgers, and the Rams calling the city home. Surrounded by mountains and hemmed in by the Pacific Ocean, there's also plenty of outdoor activities on offer.

In addition to top baseball, basketball, and American football teams, the city hosts major ice hockey and soccer franchises. Surfing is a way of life in LA, but sailing, horseback riding, biking, hiking, and golf are all available too.

SPECTATOR SPORTS

You can experience America's favorite summer pastime by grabbing a hot dog and a beer and rooting for the Dodgers baseball team at Dodger Stadium (www.mlb.com/dodgers), just north of Downtown in Chavez Ravine.

From October to April it's basketball season, when both the Lakers and the Clippers run the court at the Downtown Staples Center (www.staplescenter.com). The Los Angeles Sparks (sparks.wnba.com) of the Women's National Basketball Association also play here.

LA was without a pro American football franchise between 1994 and 2016, when the Los Angeles Rams (therams.com) arrived from St Louis – temporarily based at the Los Angeles Memorial Coliseum, they plan to move into the brand new Los Angeles Stadium in Inglewood in 2020. NFL's the Chargers (www.chargers.com) moved back to LA in 2017; they will play at the StubHub Center before also moving to the new stadium.

College football games (Aug–Dec) are as entertaining as NFL and AFL games. UCLA plays at the Rose Bowl (www.rosebowlstadium.com) in Pasadena, while USC games are at the Los Angeles Memorial Coliseum (www.lacoliseum.com).

Ice hockey fans can watch the Los Angeles Kings (www.nhl.com/kings) play at the Staples Center (Nov–March), while Major League Soccer's LA Galaxy (www.lagalaxy.com) play at the StubHub Center. The Galaxy competes in the annual 'El Trafico' derby against Los Angeles FC (www.lafc.com), who formed in 2018 at the Banc of California Stadium (www.bancofcaliforniastadium.com).

Golf

More than 100 golf courses are open to the public in Los Angeles (www.golf.lacity.org). The Los Angeles Open (currently 'Genesis Open') sees world-class golf champions flock to the city each February for the PGA tournament.

Exploring Venice beach on two wheels

The Toyota Grand Prix is an IndyCar Series auto race held on a street circuit in Long Beach (www.gplb.com) every April.

OUTDOOR ACTIVITIES

With exceptional year-round weather, over 72 miles (116km) of beaches, vast mountain ranges, and a hyper-athletic community, LA is the perfect place to get active.

Seaside fun is yours if you hit the coastal bike, skate, and jogging paths in Santa Monica and Venice, or from Manhattan Beach to Redondo Beach farther south. The Los Angeles segment of the Pacific Coast Bicentennial Bike Route is a popular trail. For more information, Los Angeles Bike Paths has a useful website, www.labikepaths.com.

Hiking trails abound in the Santa Monica and San Gabriel mountains. For information on local hiking trails, contact the Angeles National Forest (tel: 626-574 1613; www.fs.usda.gov/angeles). For a closer spot to check out nature, visit Griffith Park or Franklin Canyon. The best place to jog is the Hollywood Reservoir in the Hollywood Hills. A series of self-guided nature trails and some longer hiking routes wind through Will Rogers State Historic Park in the Pacific Palisades (www.parks.ca.gov/willrogers). Lake Arrowhead and Big Bear Lake, about two hours' drive east in the San Bernardino National Forest (www.fs.usda.gov/sbnf), consist of rugged mountain terrain. For information about parks and activities in the Santa Monica Mountains, call the Visitor Center at tel: 805-370 2301 or headquarters at tel: 805-370 2300 (www.nps.gov/samo).

Horseback riding is popular, too. Sunset Ranch (www.sunsetranchhollywood.com) provides guided rides through the Santa Monica Mountains.

WATER SPORTS

The Pacific coast from Santa Barbara south through Orange County is one big water playground. Beaches from Long Beach to Malibu are perfect for surfing, boogie-boarding, and swimming. Beachfront sports shops usually rent boards and can direct you toward lessons.

Meanwhile, Long Beach is a major center for boating; you can rent sailboats, dinghies, canoes, and powerboats of all sizes. Marina del Rey is another. In Orange County, Newport Beach is a base for rentals; as is Dana Point to the south. Alternatively, take a harbor cruise at Marina del Rey, San Pedro, or the Balboa Peninsula. Whale-watching expeditions are organized during the winter migrations; they leave from Marina del Rey, San Pedro, Newport Beach, and Long Beach. Jet skis can be rented in the above towns as well as in Malibu. You can rent kayaking or windsurfing equipment in Long Beach, Malibu, and Marina del Rey.

Other popular water sports include scuba diving and snorkeling. One of the best places to see underwater marine life is at Catalina Island, but equipment rental is also available in Long Beach, Redondo Beach, and Malibu.

An early mission in the Los Angeles area

HISTORY: KEY DATES

Long before Europeans appeared on the scene, Los Angeles was the domain of Native American tribes. A dusty backwater until the mid–1800s, no one could have conceived that this hot, arid place would become the glittering Los Angeles of today.

EARLY HISTORY

15,000–7,500 BC	Ice Age glaciers drive Paleo-Indian hunters southward to California from Siberia.
7,500–1,000 BC	Los Angeles area settled by the Tongva (Gabrieleños) and Chumash Native Californian tribes.

COLONIAL TIMES

1542	Juan Rodríguez Cabrillo, a Portuguese-born explorer, claims the area of southern California for the Spanish Empire.
1769	Gaspar de Portolà and Franciscan missionary Juan Crespí reach the present site of Los Angeles in August.
1771	Founding of the Mission San Gabriel Arcangel by Franciscans Fray Angel Francisco de Sonera and Fray Pedro Benito Cambon.
1781	Founding of El Pueblo de Nuestra Señora la Reina de Los Angeles de Porciúncula by 44 colonists from Mexico.
1818	The town is relocated to the present site of El Pueblo (Downtown LA).
1825	California becomes a territory of an independent Mexico.
1835	Los Angeles becomes capital of Mexican California.
1846–47	Los Angeles under siege and eventually captured by US forces during Mexican-American War.
1848	The treaty of Guadalupe Hidalgo ends the Mexican-American War. California annexed to the US.

AMERICAN STATE

1850	California becomes the 31st US State.
1853	Don Matteo Keeler plants the first orange trees.
1871	Massacre of at least 19 Chinese immigrants by a vigilante mob.

Dedication of the Hollywoodland sign, 1923

1876	First transcontinental railroad, the Southern Pacific, arrives.
1880	The University of Southern California opens.
1886	Pasadena and Santa Monica incorporated in Los Angeles County.
1888	Long Beach incorporated in Los Angeles County.
1892	Oil is discovered in downtown Los Angeles.

20TH CENTURY

1910	East Hollywood and Hollywood become part of Los Angeles.
1913	Cecil B. DeMille makes the first full-length feature film, *The Squaw Man*, in a barn near Highland and Sunset.
1914	Beverly Hills incorporated in Los Angeles County.
1918	Warner Bros Studios begins operating.
1922	Hollywood Bowl and Grauman's Egyptian Theatre open.
1923	The 'Hollywoodland' sign is erected.
1929	First Academy Awards presentation.
1932	The Summer Olympics take place in LA.
1955	Disneyland opens in Anaheim.
1958	Dodgers baseball team moves to LA; Brooklyn never forgets.
1961	Beach Boys rock group forms.
1965	The Watts riots; The Doors rock band form in Venice.
1968	Assassination of Robert F. Kennedy at the Ambassador Hotel.
1980	LA officially eclipses Chicago as the nation's second-largest city.
1984	The XXIII Olympiad is held in LA.
1992	Riots in reaction to the verdict in the Rodney King trial.
1994	The Northridge earthquake leaves 57 dead.
1995	The O.J. Simpson trial captures the world's attention.
1997	The Getty Center opens.

21ST CENTURY

2005	Democrat Antonio Villaraigosa elected LA's first Latino mayor.
2013	Democrat Eric Garcetti becomes the city's first Jewish mayor.
2015	The Broad, a new landmark contemporary art museum, opens.
2016	Los Angeles Rams become LA's first NFL team since 1994.
2017	Eric Garcetti re-elected major.
2018	The 90th Academy Awards are held, the first since Harvey Weinstein's exposé and the ensuing #MeToo campaign.

BEST ROUTES

Dancing in the Plaza

DOWNTOWN LOS ANGELES

Los Angeles was born in El Pueblo in the 18th century. Today, this historic district, along with the Art Deco City Hall, theaters on Broadway, and major galleries such as The Broad and LA MOCA, make an eclectic introduction to Downtown LA, and an enticing contrast to the forest of skyscrapers rising overhead.

DISTANCE: 2.5 miles (4km)
TIME: A full day
START: El Pueblo
END: LA Live
POINTS TO NOTE: If you're planning to visit any of the museums, avoid doing this walk on a Monday or Tuesday, as most of the sights close on one of these days. El Pueblo is easily accessible by Metro or bus (Union Station). The tour can be completed on foot, though the DASH buses that zip around Downtown follow much of the route (see page 134 or download the map at www. ladottransit.com). Try to reserve entry to The Broad (see page 35) in advance.

Downtown is where Los Angeles was founded in 1781. The exact location of the original settlement is unknown, but it was moved to the present site (and higher ground) of El Pueblo in 1818 due to flooding.

The city's historic heart has been experiencing something of a renaissance since the opening of the Staples Center in 1999, with many of its graceful old banks and hotels turned into apartments, and the enormous LA Live complex opening in 2008. It remains a diverse neighborhood however, with, in the space of a few blocks, adobe buildings and Mexican market stands, skid row (one of the highest concentrations of homeless people in the US), Japanese shopping plazas and avant-garde art galleries, high-rise corporate towers and antique movie palaces.

EL PUEBLO DE LOS ANGELES

Begin at the Mexican-style Los Angeles Plaza Park (or just 'the Plaza'), at the heart of **El Pueblo de Los Angeles ❶**, just across Alameda Street from Union Station. The site of the Spanish settlement of 1818, its few remaining early buildings evoke a strong sense of the Hispanic origins of LA – the rest is filled in with period replicas and a few modern buildings with Spanish Colonial-style facades. The old church on the western side of the plaza, Nuestra Señora Reina de los Angeles, or simply La Placita, is the city's oldest, dating from 1823.

City Hall incorporates sand from California's 58 counties and water from its 21 historic missions

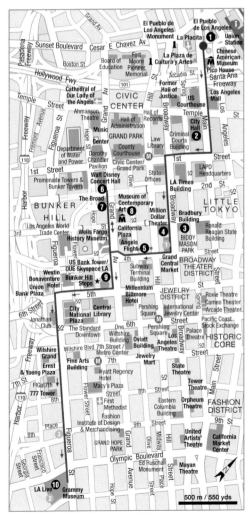

This neighborhood is covered more fully on the Pueblo tour, but if you want a taster now, pop into **La Plaza de Cultura y Artes** (see page 71) in the southwest corner of the plaza, devoted to Mexican-American culture.

Continue south along Main Street, crossing the bridge over US-101 into the Civic Center.

THE CIVIC CENTER & BROADWAY

The **Civic Center** is the governmental heart of Los Angeles. Built in 1928 (public entrance at 201 Main Street), LA's famous Art Deco **City Hall** ❷ is known to the world through LAPD badges seen in TV shows ever since *Dragnet*. Until 1960 it was the city's tallest structure (at 454ft/138 meters); it still houses the mayor's office and the Los Angeles City Council. Go up to the 27th-story observation deck for spectacular views across Downtown (www.lacity.org; Mon–Fri 9am–5pm; free).

The stunning interior of the Bradbury Building

Continue south on Main, then head right (west) on 1st Street to Broadway, passing the shiny new LAPD Headquarters and the Art Deco LA Times Building (No. 202). Walk south on Broadway for two blocks to enter the **Broadway Theater District** (aka 'Historic Downtown'). Broadway once formed the core of Los Angeles's most fashionable shopping and entertainment district, brimming with movie theaters and department stores. Today it's a bustling, slightly rundown Hispanic community, whose vendors operate out of hundred-year-old buildings, the salsa music and street culture making for one of the city's most electric environments.

The 1893 **Bradbury Building ③** at 304 South Broadway (lobby Mon–Sat 9am–5pm; free), features a magnificent sunlit atrium surrounded by wrought-iron balconies and open-cage elevators; scenes from both *Blade Runner* and *Cit-*

izen Kane* were filmed here. Opposite at No. 307 is the opulent 1918 **Million Dollar Theater ④**, built by theater magnate Sid Grauman. Next door is **Grand Central Market**, see ①, a fabulous place for lunch or a snack. Established in 1917, the indoor market sells everything from apples and oranges to *carne asada* and pickled pig's feet.

BUNKER HILL AND THE FINANCIAL DISTRICT

Exit Grand Market on the opposite (Hill Street) side and you should see the grand old **Angels Flight ⑤** funicular railway (https://angelsflight.org; daily 6.45am–10pm), rising up the steep slope to **Bunker Hill** and the **Financial District**. The original railway opened in 1901, a block north of the current location, when Bunker Hill was one of the most fashionable neighborhoods in Los Angeles. The ride is only 298ft (91 meters), but it saves an energy-sapping climb up. The railway drops you at California Plaza, just off Grand Avenue, the district's main drag. One block north, on opposite sides of the avenue, are two of the finest art museums in the city. If you have time, visit both, though you should book The Broad, which is far more popular than MOCA, in advance. Whatever you decide, make time to view the stunning **Walt Disney Concert Hall ⑥** just to the north at 111 Grand Avenue (www.musiccenter.org; 1hr self-guided audio tours most days 10am–2pm; free), a

Disney's secret garden

When visiting Walt Disney Concert Hall, don't miss the grandly titled **Walt Disney Concert Hall Community Park** (daily sunrise–sunset; free), actually a small garden and hidden gem that curves around the back of the concert hall 30ft (9 meters) above the street. Gehry's stunning **Lillian Disney Memorial Fountain** is shaped like a giant lily and covered by broken pieces of Royal Delft porcelain vases.

Walt Disney Concert Hall

Frank Gehry-designed showpiece with a titanium exterior that resembles something akin to colossal broken eggshells. Opened in 2003, it serves as the home of the Los Angeles Philharmonic Orchestra.

The Broad

The Broad ❼ (www.thebroad.org; Tue & Wed 11am–5pm, Thu & Fri 11am–8pm, Sat 10am–8pm, Sun 10am–6pm; free) opened in 2015 to house the fabulous contemporary art collection established by philanthropists Eli and Edythe Broad. It's one of LA's most popular sights, and its distinctive, metallic perforated exterior is part of the attraction. Note that the museum gets very busy at peak times (weekends in summer and all holidays), when it's worth making reservations for special exhibitions (generally $12–15) – your ticket will also allow timed entry to the permanent galleries.

The rotating permanent collection resides on the bright, futuristic third floor, with the main hall dominated by the massive cartoonish canvases of Takashi Murakami and Jeff Koons' exuberant *Tulips* installation. Koons is featured in his own gallery behind here; Robert Therrien, Jean-Michel Basquiat, Andy Warhol, Cindy Sherman, and Keith Haring are also well represented. Look out also for works by Damien Hirst, Jasper Johns, and giant canvases by Cy Twombly. But make sure to save time for Kara Walker's harrowing *African't*, a series of life-size cutouts that seem innocent enough at first glance, but which are in fact engaged in degrading acts of sex and violence representing antebellum America.

The Museum of Contemporary Art

Designed by showman architect Arata Isozaki, much of the **Museum of Contemporary Art ❽** (MOCA; www.moca.org; Mon, Wed & Fri 11am–6pm, Thu 11am–8pm, Sat & Sun 11am–5pm) is used for temporary exhibitions, but there's usually some space dedicated to the permanent collection. This comprises mostly mid-20th-century American art, particularly from the Abstract Expressionist period, including top work by usual suspects Franz Kline, Jackson Pollock, and Mark Rothko. You'll also find plenty of Pop Art and photography.

LA's tallest building

Topping out at 1,100ft (335 meters) in 2016, the **Wilshire Grand Center** at Figueroa Street and Wilshire Boulevard is now the tallest building west of the Mississippi, a massive project funded predominantly by Korean Air. The stylish steel and glass skyscraper got exemption from a city ordinance that requires all tall buildings to have helipads on the roof (for safety reasons), and instead its 18ft/5.5-meter steel spire glows with LED lights. The tower contains the spectacular InterContinental Los Angeles Downtown hotel; go up to the 70th floor lobby for sensational (and free) views, or grab a drink at the Spire Bar on the 73rd floor.

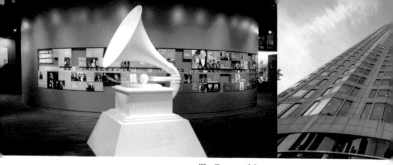

The Grammy Museum

Beyond Downtown

Just northwest of Downtown LA is Echo Park, a small oasis of palm trees and lotus blossoms set around Echo Park Lake and now one of the city's coolest neighborhoods. You can rent paddleboats or grab a drink from Beacon (www.beaconechopark.com) in the historic boathouse on the eastern edge of the lake, where you'll also see beloved Art Deco statue *Lady of the Lake*. Otherwise the neighborhood primarily appeals for its funky, bohemian atmosphere.

Historic Filipinotown (or 'Hi-Fi') covers the southwest portion of Echo Park. Highlights include the giant *Gintong Kasaysayan, Gintong Pamana* mural ('Filipino Americans: a glorious history, a golden legacy') in Unidad Park, and plenty of authentic Filipino restaurants. Just northwest of Echo Park, Silver Lake is a fashionable district that was once home to some of Hollywood's first movie studios, since converted into restaurants and galleries. The district is also known for its gay bars, quirky dance clubs, and leftist bookstores attracting plenty of hipsters and celebrities – singers Katy Perry, Beck, and Tom Waits have all lived here. Soak up the scene on Sunset Boulevard, east and west of Silver Lake Boulevard.

The Pico Union/Echo Park Dash bus runs through this neighborhood (www.ladottransit.com).

OUE Skyspace LA

From MOCA it's an easy 10-minute walk south on Grand Avenue to **US Bank Tower** and its **OUE Skyspace LA** ❾ observation deck (https://oue-skyspace.com; daily 10am–10pm). The views at sunset are magnificent. The US Bank Tower (1,018ft/310 meters), completed in 1989 at 633 W 5th Street, was the tallest building on the West Coast until 2016. For an extra $8 you can slip down a death-defying transparent glass slide attached to the outside of the building between the 70th and 69th floors. The cylindrical tower features Lawrence Halprin's huge Bunker Hill Steps at its base, supposedly modeled after the Spanish Steps in Rome.

LA LIVE

From US Bank Tower it's a 20-minute walk to the end of the tour at the **LA Live** ❿ mall complex (www.lalive.com). Walk west along 5th Street, taking in the Art Deco **Los Angeles Public Library** at No. 630, turn left on Figueroa and continue six blocks south (take a taxi, or Dash bus F on Flower Street at 5th, if you don't want to walk).

The **Grammy Museum** (www.grammymuseum.org; Mon–Fri 10.30am–6.30pm, Sat & Sun 10am–6.30pm) here is especially entertaining for kids. The museum is not just devoted to all things Grammy Awards (usually held in the on-site Microsoft Theater in February), but recorded music in gen-

Lofty OUE Skyspace LA

Eating at Grand Central Market

eral, with interactive displays over four floors including the Songwriters Hall of Fame, stage outfits and exhibits on Ray Charles and Sam Cooke, personal artifacts from Elvis Presley, Miles Davis, and Neil Diamond, and a real recording studio.

LA Live itself is a $2.5-billion shopping and entertainment complex that features movie theaters, sports facilities and broadcast studios, upper-end hotels, a central plaza, a bowling alley, and numerous arcades and restaurants where you have plenty of choice for dinner, such as **Wolfgang Puck Bar & Grill**, see ②. Alternatively, the **Original Pantry Café**, see ③, one block north on South Figueroa Street, is a classic LA diner open 24 hours.

The History of California

If you have time, pop in to the **LA Public Library** (Mon–Thu 10am–8pm, Fri & Sat 9.30am–5.30pm, Sun 1–5pm; free) to view the sensational murals inside the Grand Rotunda. Dubbed the *History of California*, the vast 12-panel series was completed in 1933 by American artist Dean Cornwell. It took him five years to complete the project, painting the murals on fine Belgium linen. Cornwell's panels cover four areas of California history: *The Era of Discovery, The Missions, Americanization*, and *The Founding of the city of Los Angeles*. The library building itself is an Art Deco stunner completed in 1926, topped with a distinctive tiled mosaic pyramid.

Food and Drink

① GRAND CENTRAL MARKET

317 S Broadway; tel: 213-624 2378; www.grandcentralmarket.com; daily 8am–10pm; $

Venerable food market, with tempting options including the China Café (daily 9am–10pm), breakfast specialist Eggslut (daily 8am–4pm), Horse Thief BBQ (daily 11am–10pm), and Sarita's Pupuseria (daily 9am–6pm) for Salvadorean *pupusas* (stuffed tortillas).

② WOLFGANG PUCK BAR & GRILL

LA Live, 800 W Olympic Boulevard; tel: 213-748 9700; www.wolfgangpuck.com; Mon & Sun 5–10pm, Tue–Sat 11.30am–11pm; $$

One of the more affordable restaurants in the Puck stable, serving contemporary American lunch and dinner menus with innovative takes on traditional comfort foods.

③ ORIGINAL PANTRY CAFÉ

877 S Figueroa St; tel: 213-972 9279; www.pantrycafe.com; daily 24hr; $

Hearty portions of meaty American cooking – chops and steaks, mostly – since 1924, in this diner owned by former mayor Dick Riordan. The breakfast is the best option (available all day); plates start at just $5.50. Rapid service and huge plates. Cash only.

The Hollywood & Highland Center

HOLLYWOOD

Known the world over for the movies and the glamorous life associated with it, Hollywood attracts millions of tourists every year. The area contains some major LA icons; this walking tour takes in the Chinese Theatre, Hollywood Walk of Fame, and Paramount Studios all in one day.

DISTANCE: 3 miles (4.8km)
TIME: A full day
START: Hollywood/Highland Station (LA Metro)
END: Hollywood/Vine (LA Metro) or Paramount Studios
POINTS TO NOTE: This tour is especially fun for kids, with Hollywood Boulevard lined with family-friendly attractions. The main route is an easy stroll, bookended by two Metro stations. The cemetery/Paramount Studios extension is a longer hike or taxi ride. If you plan on touring Paramount Studios, purchase tickets in advance (www.paramountstudiotour.com).

Strangely enough, Hollywood started life in the 1880s as a temperance colony, created to be a sober, God-fearing alternative to raunchy Downtown LA. But then came the movie-makers, lured by cheap labor, low taxes, and guaranteed sunshine.

Hollywood continues to be a secondary center for the movie business, but all the big film companies (other than

Paramount) relocated long ago. Things have brightened up in the past few years, however, as prolonged efforts by local authorities have successfully reversed the decline that blighted the area from the early 1960s. The contrasting qualities of freshly polished nostalgia, corporate hype, and seediness make Hollywood one of LA's most diverse areas – and one of its best spots for bar-hopping and clubbing.

HOLLYWOOD & HIGHLAND CENTER

Start at the contemporary heart of downtown Hollywood, the **Hollywood**

The Oscars

The **Academy Awards** (www.oscars.org) are usually presented in March at a star-studded ceremony in the Dolby Theatre on Hollywood Boulevard. The tradition began back in 1929, at the Hollywood Roosevelt Hotel, when just 15 statuettes were awarded.

Star-gazing at the Oscars

& Highland Center ❶ (www.hollywood andhighland.com) shopping mall and the **Dolby Theatre** (www.dolbytheatre. com; tours daily 10.30am–4pm, every 30 mins), home of the Oscars. Stores open at 10am, but spots like Kelly's Coffee & Fudge Factory and Johnny Rockets should be serving breakfast much earlier.

TCL Chinese Theatre

Part of the center complex and one of the neighborhood's most famous sights is the **TCL Chinese Theatre ❷** (www. tclchinesetheatres.com; tours daily 10am–8.30pm, every 15–30 mins). The theater opened in 1927 and has now expanded into a multiplex, its main auditorium restored to its glori-

Waxwork at Madame Tussauds

ously kitschy origins. This was one of Sid Grauman's showpieces from the early days of the movie biz, an odd version of a classical Asian temple, replete with dubious Chinese motifs and upturned dragon-tail flanks. You'll probably encounter celebrity impersonators outside, plus low-rent magicians, smiling hawkers, and assorted oddballs, all vying for your amusement and money.

Madame Tussauds Hollywood

Just beyond the Chinese Theatre, **Madame Tussauds Hollywood** (www.madametussauds.com/hollywood; daily 10am–7pm) is tucked in to the western side of the Hollywood & Highland Center. This branch is quite a spectacle, with a vast array of scarily life-like wax models representing the gamut of Hollywood movies, from Westerns to Marvel superheroes, with US sports heroes thrown in for good measure.

> ## The Rock Walk
>
> Around one mile (1.6km) southwest of Hollywood and Highland is the celebrated **Guitar Center Hollywood** (stores.guitarcenter.com/hollywood). This vast musical-instrument store features the **Rock Walk**, with handprints of over 400 of your favorite guitar gods embedded in the manner of the movie stars' at the Chinese Theatre, in this case with performers from AC/DC and ZZ Top to The Cure and Les Paul.

El Capitan Theatre

Cross to the south side of Hollywood Boulevard and head back east, passing the **El Capitan Theatre ❸** (https://elcapitantheatre.com). This colorful 1926 movie palace features a Spanish Baroque and Moorish facade and a wild South Seas-themed interior of sculpted angels and garlands. The theater also has one of LA's great signs, a multicolored profusion of flashing bulbs and neon tubes. Today it hosts Disney premieres (Disney owns it). The old Masonic Temple next door hosts the TV talk show of comedian **Jimmy Kimmel** (which tapes at 4pm Mon–Thu; for free tickets visit https://1iota.com), while on the other side of the theater kids will go gaga for the **Disney Studio Store and Ghirardelli Soda Fountain** (Mon–Thu & Sun 10.30am–10pm, Fri & Sat 10.30am–11pm).

Hollywood Museum

Keeping walking east along Hollywood Boulevard to Highlands for a short detour south to the **Hollywood Museum ❹** (thehollywoodmuseum.com; Wed–Sun 10am–5pm). Inside, exhibits explore the fashion, art design, props, and special effects taken from a broad swath of movie history, including the *Harry Potter* series. Given that this is the old Max Factor Building (1935), there's also a reproduction of Max Factor's movie make-up rooms, where Marilyn Monroe turned into a blonde (she was naturally a brunette). The permanent collection includes Mon-

TCL Chinese Theatre

Ripley's Believe It or Not!

roe's million-dollar honeymoon dress, make-up bag, and Springolator high heels, Elvis' bathrobe, Rocky's boxing gloves, and Hannibal Lecter's entire prison cell from *Silence of the Lambs*.

HOLLYWOOD BOULEVARD

Retrace your steps to Hollywood Boulevard and continue east from Highland; by now you will have seen evidence of the **Hollywood Walk of Fame** (www. walkoffame.com) on either side of the street. Comprising over 2,500 pink terrazzo and brass stars embedded in the sidewalks along 15 blocks of Hollywood Boulevard and three blocks of Vine, the Walk of Fame was initiated in 1960. It honors the big names in radio, television, movies, music, and theater: among them are Audrey Hepburn (1606 Vine Street), Johnny Depp (7020 Hollywood Boulevard), and Elvis Presley (6777 Hollywood Boulevard). Look out for the unique moon-shaped monuments to the Apollo 11 mission, at the corners of Hollywood and Vine.

The first block east of Highland Avenue contains three kitsch attractions, though kids may find them entertaining. The Hollywood branch of the ubiquitous **Ripley's Believe It or Not!** ❺ (www. ripleys.com/hollywood; daily 10am–midnight) is the most fun, containing two floors of more than 300 wacky exhibits, including shrunken heads and two-headed goats. Next door, the **Guinness World Records Museum**

(www.guinnessmuseumhollywood. com; Mon–Thu 9am–midnight, Fri–Sat until 1am) is housed in the historic Hollywood Theater, opened in 1913 and given a gorgeous Art Deco makeover in 1938. Across the street at No. 6767, the **Hollywood Wax Museum** (www. hollywoodwaxmuseum.com; Sun–Thu 9am–midnight, Fri & Sat 9am–1am) is crammed full of life-sized re-creations of movie stars, though Madame Tussauds is better.

Chinese Theatre prints

The **TCL Chinese Theatre** was for many decades *the* spot for movie first nights, and the public crowded behind the rope barriers in their thousands to glimpse the stars. The main draw today is the assortment of **cement handprints and footprints** embedded in the theater's forecourt. The idea came about when actress Norma Talmadge trod in wet cement while visiting the construction site with owner Sid Grauman. The first formally to leave their marks were Mary Pickford and Douglas Fairbanks Sr, who ceremoniously dipped their digits when arriving for the opening of *King of Kings* in 1927, and the practice continues today. It's certainly fun to work out the actual dimensions of your favorite film stars, and to discover if your hands are smaller than Julie Andrews' or your feet bigger than Rock Hudson's.

At night, the light at the top of the Capitol Records Building blinks out 'Hollywood' in Morse code

Egyptian Theatre

The **Egyptian Theatre** ❻ (americancine mathequecalendar.com; tours once a month, Sat 10.30am) was the site of the very first Hollywood premiere (*Robin Hood*, an epic swashbuckler starring Douglas Fairbanks Sr) in 1922. Financed by impresario Sid Grauman, the Egyptian was a glorious fantasy in its heyday, modestly seeking to re-create the Temple of Thebes, with usherettes dressed as Cleopatra. It has since been lovingly restored and plays an assortment of classics, documentaries, avant-garde flicks, and foreign films. It's a short walk east along Hollywood Boulevard from here to legendary **Musso & Frank Grill**, see ❶, a great place for lunch or an afternoon tipple.

HOLLYWOOD & VINE

From the Egyptian Theatre it's a half-mile (800 meters) or so along Hollywood Boulevard to Hollywood and Vine, the nexus for an especially heavy dose

Hollywood Farmers' Market

Lining Ivar Avenue and Selma Avenue, between Sunset and Hollywood boulevards, the popular **Hollywood Farmers' Market** (www.hollywoodfarmersmarket. net; Sun 8am–1pm) features over 100 vendors selling a variety of produce, from local citrus fruits and avocados to more exotic specimens like cherimoyas.

of redevelopment, led by the opening of the mammoth W Hollywood Hotel in 2010. Along the way, book lovers will want to stop at **Larry Edmunds Bookshop** ❼ (larryedmunds.com; Mon–Fri 10am–5.30pm, Sat 10am–6pm, Sun noon–5.30pm) for movie books and posters. Art aficionados should take a peek inside **LACE** ❽ at No. 6522 (Los Angeles Contemporary Exhibitions; welcometolace.org; Wed–Sun noon–6pm).

Looking north along Vine Street you can see the iconic **Capitol Records Building** ❾ (at No. 1750), resembling a stack of 45rpm vinyl records and serving as the music company's headquarters since 1956 (it was sold to a developer in 2006, but Capitol continues to use the building as its West Coast office). Across the street, **Hollywood Burger**, see ❷, is a great spot for a quick bite or early evening meal.

HOLLYWOOD FOREVER CEMETERY

If you still have time, walk south (20 minutes) or jump into a taxi at Hollywood and Vine for the short ride (1 mile/1.6km) to the **Hollywood Forever Cemetery** ❿ (6000 Santa Monica Boulevard; www.hollywoodforever.com; grounds Mon–Fri 8.30am–5pm, Sat & Sun 8.30am–5.30pm; free; tours Sat 10am). Founded in 1899 and overlooked by the famous water tower of neighboring Paramount Studios, the cemetery displays myriad tombs of dead celeb-

Iconic Musso & Frank Grill

rities, most notably in its southeastern corner, where the Cathedral Mausoleum includes, at No. 1205, the resting place of Rudolph Valentino. In 1926, 10,000 people packed the cemetery when the celebrated screen lover died aged just 31. If you visit in the summer, don't miss Cinespia (www.cinespia.org), when thousands come with beach chairs, blankets, beer, wine (no spirits allowed), and food to sit on the Fairbanks Lawn and watch classic movies projected onto the wall of the mausoleum.

SIDE TRIP: PARAMOUNT STUDIOS

If you skip the kitschy attractions on Hollywood Boulevard, you should have time for **Paramount Studios** ⑪ (www.paramountstudiotour.com; tours daily 9am–4pm, every 15–30 mins); alterna-tively, consider the 'After Dark Tour' which runs Thursday, Friday, and Saturday evenings. One of the few true movie-making attractions remaining in Hollywood, Paramount Studios were built in 1917 as the Peralta Studios and purchased by their current owner in 1926. The original iconic arched entrance – which Gloria Swanson rode through in *Sunset Boulevard* – is now inside the complex opposite Bronson Avenue (you can just about see it from Melrose Avenue), but the only way to get inside the 65-acre (26-hectare) lot is on a guided tour. The tours are not quite the standard of Universal's theme-park madness or Warner Bros' close-up journey, but if you want to poke around sound stages and classic backlots, it's definitely worth it. If you end up down here, **Lucy's El Adobe Café**, see ③, is a classic Mexican spot for dinner.

Food and Drink

① MUSSO & FRANK GRILL
6667 Hollywood Boulevard; tel: 323-467 7788; www.mussoandfrank.com; Tue–Sat 11am–11pm, Sun 4–9pm; $$$
If you haven't had a drink in this 1919 landmark bar, you haven't been to Hollywood. It serves pricey diner food as well as an array of steaks, sandwiches, and Italian dishes.

② HOLLYWOOD BURGER
6250 Hollywood Boulevard; tel: 323-378 5668; www.hollywood-burger.com; daily 8am–10pm; $
A cut above the average fast-food joint, with gourmet burgers made to order and served on a tasty potato bun.

③ LUCY'S EL ADOBE CAFÉ
5536 Melrose Avenue; tel: 323-462 9421; daily 11.30am–11pm; $
No-frills Mexican diner since 1964, though matriarch Lucy Casado died at the age of 91 in 2017. Enjoy a delicious plate of *mole poblano*, chili verde, or tacos, washed down with the best margaritas in town.

Muscle Beach Venice

VENICE, SANTA MONICA, AND MALIBU

For many, the progressive beachside communities of Malibu, Santa Monica, and Venice are the best parts of LA, with swaths of white sand, palms, hip restaurants and stores, and a fiercely independent surf culture made famous by bands like The Doors.

DISTANCE: 3-mile (4.8km) walk from Venice to Santa Monica, followed by a 12-mile (19.3km) bus ride to Malibu (via Getty Villa)
TIME: A full day
START: Venice Pier
END: Adamson House/Malibu Pier
POINTS TO NOTE: There is a parking lot at Venice Pier, but several bus routes will drop you here; the Metro goes as far as Santa Monica, where it's easy to get buses to Venice Beach. Be sure to bring plenty of water and sunscreen – the ocean breezes can be cooling, but the sun is very powerful. The Getty Villa is closed Tuesdays; make sure you book a timed-entry ticket in advance at www.getty.edu.

Friendly and liberal, Santa Monica is a great place to visit, a compact, accessible bastion of oceanside charm. Most of its attractions lie within a few blocks of the beach and Palisades Park, the famous, cypress-tree-lined strip that runs along the top of the bluffs and makes for striking views of the surf below.

Immediately south of Santa Monica, Venice is the eccentric, loopy version of Los Angeles, home to outlandish skaters, brazen bodybuilders, panhandlers, streetballers, street musicians, and street-side comedians. The neighborhood gained its bohemian reputation in the 1950s and 1960s, when the Beats and then bands like The Doors bummed around the beach. Though gentrification has definitely had an impact in recent years, Venice retains an edgy feel in parts.

VENICE BEACH

Start the route bright and early at **Venice Pier** ❶, the southern hub of the beach boardwalk at the western end of busy Washington Boulevard. The 1,300ft (396-meter) pier was built in 1963, offering a scenic viewpoint back along the coast. You can grab breakfast nearby at **Hinano Café**, see ❶, a classic beach-shack diner.

Walk north along the boardwalk from the pier, soaking up the scene. Stretching for around three miles (4.8km), the

Riding the surf

Venice–Santa Monica Beach Boardwalk is Southern California's number one visitor attraction. The path splits just north of the pier, with the westerly arm taking a more winding route across the beach itself, and the eastern branch running straight up the shoreline. The latter is where you'll see hundreds of street vendors and performers, breakdancers, artists, and tattoo parlors; nowhere else does LA parade itself quite so openly and colorfully. Year-round on weekends and every day in summer it's packed with jugglers, fire-eaters, Hare Krishnas, rasta guitar players and, of course, teeming masses of tourists. Rollerbladers, skateboarders, volleyball players, and cyclists are also ubiquitous.

Muscle Beach Venice

At 19th Avenue you'll come to **Muscle Beach Venice ❷** (www.musclebeachvenice.com), a legendary weightlifting 'pen' where serious hunks of muscle pump serious iron. Muscle Beach was originally established on the sands just south of Santa Monica Pier in 1933, with this section opening in 1951. Behind Muscle Beach, on parallel Speedway (nip down 19th Avenue and turn left along the alley), two giant **murals** adorn the house at No. 1822: Arnold Schwarzenegger in full muscle mode (created by artist Jonas Never in 2013); and Doors frontman Jim Morrison in his 1960s heyday, by famed Venice muralist Rip Cronk in 1991 (and given a makeover in 2012).

A little farther north along the boardwalk, at Windward Avenue, turn right to view the **Venice Sign ❸** in lights, hanging across the street (Windward at Pacific Avenue, 1 block inland). The sign is a 2007 replica of the one originally installed in 1905 by Venice founder Abbot Kinney.

Windward Avenue

Windward Avenue is the main artery of Venice, running from the beach into what was the Grand Circle of the canal system (now paved over). The original Romanesque arcade, around the intersection with Pacific Avenue, is alive with health-food stores, trinket shops, and rollerblade rental stands. Before continuing north on the boardwalk, check

Lords of Dogtown

In the 1970s the district around the ruined Pacific Ocean Park on the south side of Santa Monica was known as **Dogtown**. It was here in the early 1970s that a group of surfers and skateboarders known as the **Z-boys** revolutionized skateboarding; in 1977 member Tony Alva 'invented' the first aerial. Though the Z-boys soon split up, their story was fictionalized in the 2005 movie *Lords of Dogtown*, and the location of their Zephyr surf shop (long since closed) at 2003 Main Street is protected as a City Landmark; it's now occupied by **Dogtown Coffee** (Mon–Fri 5.30am–5pm, Sat & Sun 6.30am–5pm).

out Cronk's 1989 *Venice Reconstituted* mural, nicknamed 'Botticelli's *Venus* on rollerskates' (Windward at Speedway).

As the boardwalk gets closer to Santa Monica the vendors and beach bars give way to a quieter stretch of landscaped parks lined with palms and posh condos. You can continue all the way to Santa Monica Pier, or take a break from the beach and head inland

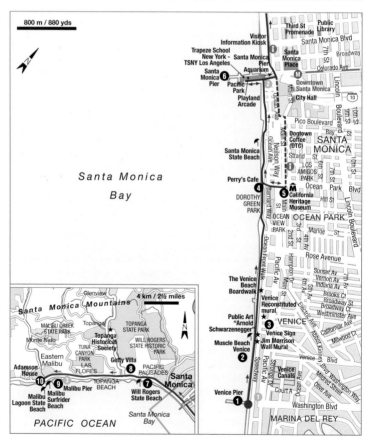

Prime real estate: Santa Monica's colorful beach houses

at **Perry's Café** ❹, strolling east along Ocean Park Boulevard.

SANTA MONICA

Two blocks inland from the beach, Santa Monica's **Main Street** is an enticing collection of boutiques, bars, and restaurants that forms one of the most popular shopping strips on the Westside. The **California Heritage Museum** ❺ (www. californiaheritagemuseum.org; Wed–Sun 11am–4pm) at 2612 Main Street hosts temporary displays on Californian cultural topics, from old fruit-box labels to modern skateboards, and has permanent exhibits on regional pottery, furniture, quilts, and decorative arts. The building itself is as interesting as the exhibits, a Queen Anne-style gem built in 1894 by lauded architect Sumner P. Hunt for Roy Jones, son of the founder of Santa Monica. From here you can double back along Ocean Park Boulevard and continue along the beach to Santa Monica Pier, or continue north along Main Street for around one mile (1.6km) to Colorado Avenue, the main road leading to the pier.

Santa Monica Pier

Jutting out into the bay at the foot of Colorado Avenue, **Santa Monica Pier** ❻ (https://santamonicapier.org) is an iconic example of an old-fashioned, festive beach-town hub, dating back to 1909 and featuring in numerous movies with its giant rollercoaster, Ferris wheel, and restored 1922 wooden Carousel. Other family-friendly attractions include the **Trapeze School** (www. trapezeschool.com), **Playland Arcade** (Mon–Thu 10am–10pm, Fri & Sat 10am–1am, Sun 10am–midnight), and the thrill rides of **Pacific Park** (www.pacpark.com; seasonal hours, check website). The **Santa Monica Pier Aquarium**, below the pier at 1600 Ocean Front Walk (https://healthebay. org/aquarium; seasonal hours, check website), is where you can find out about marine biology and touch sea anemones and starfish. The pier area features plenty of places to grab lunch or a snack, including **Big Dean's Ocean Front Café**, see ❷ .

Third Street Promenade

If you've had enough of the sun and sand, head inland from Santa Monica Pier along Colorado Avenue to Santa Monica Place mall and the Third Street Promenade, a three-block pedestrian-only shopping street that's one of LA's most densely touristed, especially on summer weekends. The promenade gets busy at night, when huge numbers of visitors and locals jostle for space with sidewalk poets and swinging jazz bands under the watchful eyes of water-spewing dinosaur sculptures draped in ivy. Santa Monica Place, a lively outdoor retail complex, anchors the southern end of the Promenade.

THE GETTY VILLA

From Santa Monica Pier the beach continues in a golden ribbon for another 3.5 miles (5.6km) north to **Will Rogers State Beach ❼**, but the main attraction up here is the **Getty Villa ❽** (17985 Pacific Coast Highway, Pacific Palisades; getty.edu; Wed–Mon 10am–5pm; free by advance ticket only), some two miles (3.2km) farther along. From Santa Monica Pier the easiest option is to take the No. 543 bus (every 20 mins from Ocean and Colorado), which makes the trip in around 15 min-

utes, and drops you off on the main highway just below the villa entrance (visitors must have the bus driver hole-punch their villa ticket in order to enter the sight; if arriving by taxi, get a taxi receipt).

The Getty Villa was built by oil tycoon J. Paul Getty in 1974 adjacent to his home in Pacific Palisades, serving as the original Getty museum until the current center was completed (see page 89). It now serves as the Getty Foundation's spectacular showcase for its wide array of Greek, Etruscan, and Roman antiquities. Modeled on a Roman country house buried by Mount Vesuvius in AD 79, the museum is built around its own fetching gardens, peppered with replicas of stern-looking Roman heads.

The rooms in the Getty Villa are grouped in themes ranging from religious and mythic to theatrical to martial. Highlights include the *Getty Kouros*, a rigidly posed figure of a boy that conservators openly admit could be a later forgery, as well as Athenian vases.

MALIBU

Everyone has heard of **Malibu**; it's been immortalized in surfing movies since the 1960s, Courtney Love sung about it, and it served as the fictional home of Hannah Montana, *Two and a Half Men*, and *Iron Man*. While its pop, Hollywood image is not so very far from the truth, you might not think so on arrival. The succession of ramshackle surf shops and fast-food stands scattered along both sides of

Malibu's surf scene

Though Polynesians and especially Hawaiians have been surfing for hundreds of years, modern surf culture really went mainstream on LA beaches (particularly Malibu) in the late 1950s. Movies such as *Gidget* (1959), filmed on Malibu's Surfrider Beach and in Leo Carrillo State Park, sparked a flood of interest and instigated the genre known as beach party films (1963's *Beach Party* was also filmed in Malibu), as well as the surf music of Dick Dale, the **Beach Boys** (formed in nearby Hawthorne, LA, in 1961), and others. It wasn't all fun though; environmentalism has always been a key aspect of surf culture, and the **Surfrider Foundation** (www.surfrider.org) was formed in Malibu in 1984 by surfers to protest threats to their local breaks – it's now a global activist movement.

The picture-perfect Getty Villa

Pacific Coast Highway (PCH) around the graceful Malibu Pier don't exactly reek of money, but the secluded estates just inland are as valuable as any: Halle Berry, Lady Gaga, John McEnroe, Steven Spielberg, and Barbara Streisand are among numerous stars that have homes here. From the Getty Villa you can simply walk back down to the main highway and take the next No. 543 bus (every 15–20 mins) west to **Malibu Pier** ❾ (around 20 mins).

Malibu Lagoon State Beach

The main attraction here, just beyond the pier, is **Malibu Lagoon State Beach** and its celebrated **Surfrider Beach**, which first gained recognition when the sport was brought over from Hawaii and mastered by Southern California pioneers.

The waves are best in late summer, when storms off Mexico cause them to reach upward of 8ft (2.5 meters) – not huge for serious pros, but big enough for amateurs. Nearby is the **Adamson House** ❿ (23200 Pacific Coast Highway; www. adamsonhouse.org; Fri & Sat 11am–3pm by tour, last one at 2pm), a stunning, historic Spanish Revival-style home built in 1929, featuring opulent decor and colorful 'Malibu Potteries' tile work. The adjoining **Malibu Lagoon Museum** (details as above), formerly the Adamsons' five-car garage, chronicles the history of the area from the days of the Chumash people to the 'gentlemen' ranchers and the birth of modern surfing. End the day with a cold beer on the pier, or head to **Nobu Malibu**, see ❸, for something special.

Food and Drink

❶ HINANO CAFÉ

15 W Washington Boulevard, Venice; tel: 310-822 3902; www.hinanocafevenice.com; daily 8am–2am; $

Chilled beach shack with pool tables, good and cheap burgers, shambling decor, and a mostly local crowd. Open since 1962, this was, allegedly, Jim Morrison's local. Cash only.

❷ BIG DEAN'S OCEAN FRONT CAFÉ

1615 Ocean Front Walk, Santa Monica; tel: 310-393 2666; www. bigdeansoceanfrontcafe.com; Mon noon–9pm, Tue & Wed 11am–9pm, Thu & Fri 11am–11pm, Sat 10am–11pm, Sun 10am–10pm; $$

Local institution by the pier since the 1970s, with great food, beer, sports on 17 TVs, and outdoor patios. Think buffalo wings, grilled hamburgers, and hot dogs.

❸ NOBU MALIBU

22706 Pacific Coast Highway; tel: 310-317 9140; www.noburestaurants.com; Mon–Thu noon–10pm, Fri & Sat 9am–11pm, Sun 9am–10pm; $$$

This is what you expect in Malibu: amazing ocean views, romantic setting, and the celeb chef's top-notch seafood (black cod miso, yellowtail sashimi).

BEVERLY HILLS

One of the world's most exclusive neighborhoods, Beverly Hills has been synonymous with Hollywood glamor since the 1950s, the home of opulent mansions and the celebrities who own them, as well as the high-end boutiques and restaurants of Rodeo Drive.

DISTANCE: 2-mile (3.2km) walk to Beverly Hills Hotel, followed by a 1.3-mile (2km) taxi ride to Greystone Mansion
TIME: A full day
START: Beverly Wilshire
END: Greystone Mansion
POINTS TO NOTE: Metro Rapid Line bus No. 720 and Metro Local Line bus No. 20 run along Wilshire Boulevard to Beverly Hills. Once here, most of the route can be completed easily on foot, but taxis will be required to and from Greystone Mansion.

Beverly Hills Trolley

If you just have time for a quick overview of the Beverly Hills shopping scene, take a trip on the free **Beverly Hills Trolley** between Civic Center and Rodeo Drive. The trolley departs hourly (Jan–June & Sept–Nov Sat & Sun 11am–4pm, July, Aug, & Dec Tue–Sun 11am–5pm).

Think Beverly Hills, think free-spending wealth and untrammeled luxury. This millionaire mecca has been home to some of America's biggest stars since the 1950s: Jennifer Aniston, Ray Charles, Jennifer Lawrence, Elvis Presley, Frank Sinatra, and Elizabeth Taylor among them.

The city remains independent (it's part of Los Angeles County, but not LA itself), and divides into two distinct halves, separated by Santa Monica Boulevard. To the south is the flashy Golden Triangle business district, ground zero for window-shopping and gawking at major and minor celebrities, while to the north lies the tranquil, very exclusive residential area.

RODEO DRIVE

Begin at the southern end of **Rodeo Drive** at the **Beverly Wilshire ❶** (9500 Wilshire Boulevard; www.fourseasons.com). Open since 1928, this palatial hotel featured in the 1990 hit movie *Pretty Woman*. For the full experience, have a luxurious breakfast (served 6.30–11.30am) at **THE Boulevard** restaurant (theblvdrestaurant.

com) inside, or for something cheaper, nip around the corner to **Chaumont Bakery & Café**, see .

Retail heaven

From the Beverly Wilshire, Rodeo Drive cuts north through the Golden Triangle in a two-block-long showcase of the most expensive names in international fashion. It's a dauntingly stylish area, each boutique trying to outshine the rest, crowned by **Two Rodeo ❷** at Wilshire, a faux-European shopping alley – look for the steps next to Tiffany & Co opposite the hotel and stroll north along this pedestrian-only mall.

Two Rodeo mall rejoins Rodeo Drive at Dayton, where Robert Graham's *Torso* sculpture in the middle of the street marks the southern end of the **Rodeo Drive Walk of Style**. Initiated in 2003 and modeled on Hollywood's Walk of Fame, plaques on the sidewalk (on both sides of the street) honor all the big names in fashion, beginning with Giorgio Armani. Also at Rodeo and Dayton, you can't miss the incredibly stylish **Louis Vuitton ❸** boutique (Mon–Sat 10am–7pm, Sun 11am–6pm), its facade comprising louver-like stainless steel ribbons over glass. Just to the north, the equally chic **Dior ❹** flagship houses its signature purse collection, as well as shoes, clothing, makeup, sunglasses, and jewelry.

As you continue walking north on Rodeo, check out the **Anderton Court Shops ❺** complex at No. 332, the last LA building by famed architect Frank Lloyd Wright, completed in 1952 with its trademark 'steeple' on top. Next door at No. 346, the beautiful **Tom Ford** boutique is also worth visiting, as is **Roberto Cavalli** at No. 362. At Brighton Way you'll see the distinctive **Chanel ❻** flagship boutique (Mon–Sat 10am–6pm, Sun noon–5pm), which contains a two-story video wall playing Chanel fashion shows. At No. 420 look for the **House of Bijan,** a legendary by-appointment-only showroom inside a lavish Mediterranean-style golden palazzo; the designer's Bijan Rolls-Royce Phantom Drophead Coupe, one of the world's most expensive cars (along with a yellow Bugatti) is often parked outside by the yellow-painted parking meter.

Continue to South Santa Monica Boulevard and turn right, walking two short blocks to North Beverly Drive. En route, visitors with a sweet tooth should check out **Sugarfina** (9495 S Santa

---

The Sprinkles cupcakes 'ATM'

Turn left on South Santa Monica Boulevard at Rodeo Drive and walk two blocks west to No. 9635 to see one of the quirkier Beverly Hills sights. Next door to the actual Sprinkles store, this multicolored cupcake vending machine really does look like an ATM. Use the touchscreen to order a freshly baked red velvet, chocolate marshmallow, or vanilla peppermint 24-hours a day (credit cards only).

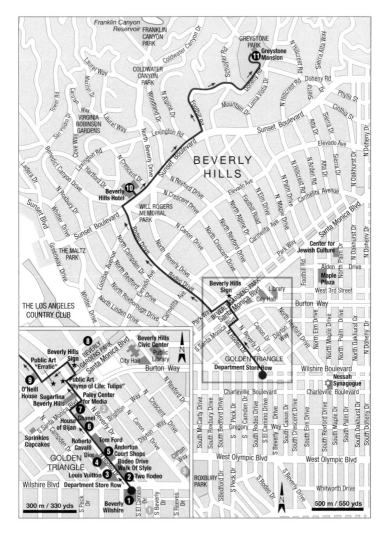

Greystone
Park

11 Greystone Mansion

Franklin Canyon
Reservoir

FRANKLIN
CANYON
PARK

COLDWATER
CANYON
PARK

VIRGINIA
ROBINSON
GARDENS

BEVERLY
HILLS

Sunset Boulevard

10 Beverly
Hills Hotel

WILL ROGERS
MEMORIAL
PARK

THE MALTZ
PARK

THE LOS ANGELES
COUNTRY CLUB

Center for
Jewish Culture

Maple
Plaza

West 3rd Street

Burton Way

Beverly Hills
Sign

Library

City Hall

GOLDEN TRIANGLE
Department Store Row

Wilshire Boulevard

Nessah
Synagogue

Charleville Boulevard

West Olympic Blvd

ROXBURY
PARK

Whitworth Drive

500 m / 550 yds

8

BEVERLY
GARDENS PARK

Beverly Hills
Sign

Public Art
"Erratic"

9

O'Neill
House

Public Art
"Hymn of Life: Tulips"

Paley Center
for Media

Sugarfina
Beverly Hills

7

Chanel

House
of Bijan

6

Roberto
Cavalli

Tom Ford

Dior

Anderton
Court Shops

Rodeo Drive
Walk Of Style

Sprinkles
Cupcakes

5

4

Louis Vuitton

3

GOLDEN
TRIANGLE

2

Two Rodeo

Wilshire Blvd   Department Store Row

1

Beverly
Wilshire

Beverly Hills
Civic Center

Public
Library

Burton Way

300 m / 330 yds

N

The Beverly Hills Sign

Monica Boulevard), a beautifully curated candy store.

PALEY CENTER FOR MEDIA

The entertaining **Paley Center for Media ❼** (465 N Beverly Drive; tel: 310-786 1000; www.paleycenter.org; Wed–Sun noon–5pm; free) features a collection of more than 160,000 television and radio programs. It also presents rotating exhibits on famous TV characters from the 20th century, and the best of radio and TV sitcoms, dramas, and thrillers. The video archive of Olympic Games television coverage – spanning the televised history of the games from the 1960 Winter Games in Squaw Valley – is also publicly accessible.

Check the website for upcoming programs, talks with influential newsmakers, journalists, and world leaders, and special events at the Center. Afterward, walk south a half block to **Nate'n Al Delicatessen**, see ❷, for lunch or a coffee.

BEVERLY GARDENS PARK

After lunch, walk north along North Beverly Drive a couple of blocks to **Beverly Gardens Park ❽** (www.fobgp. org), a series of landscaped gardens that runs east–west for almost 2 miles (3.2km). It's the location of the annual **Beverly Hills Art Show**, held during the third weekends in May and October. The park also contains the **Beverly Hills Sign**, a much-photographed landmark (walk east from N Beverly Drive). The 40ft (12-meter) long, illuminated sign is actually a replica of the 1907 original, installed in front of a lily pond in the center of the park. The park is sprinkled throughout with bold contemporary artwork, including *Hymn of Life: Tulips* (2007), by Yayoi Kusama, and *Erratic* (2007) by Roxy Paine, an enormous, polished, stainless steel boulder. Exit the park at its northwestern corner at Rodeo Drive. On the other side of the street is the **O'Neill House ❾**, a whimsical fantasy home inspired by the Art Nouveau designs of Spanish archi-

Virginia Robinson Gardens

Tranquil **Virginia Robinson Gardens** (1008 Elden Way; www.robinsongardens. org), contains one of the few Beverly Hills mansions open to the public. The Beaux Arts-style mansion and iconic Renaissance Revival pool pavilion were built in 1911 for retail tycoons Virginia and Harry Robinson (of the Robinsons-May Department stores). Visiting involves some planning, as tours are offered Tuesday to Saturday, by reservation only (check website for current schedule or tel: 310-550 2087); tours include a walk through the antique-laden house, but mostly focus on the six botanical gardens. Virginia Robinson was known as the 'First Lady of Beverly Hills,' legendary for her card games and lavish celebrity-filled parties.

Movies filmed in the Greystone Mansion include Spider-Man and Ghostbusters

tect Antoni Gaudí. Walk down the alley that runs along the house's left side (off Park Way) to see the swirling exterior up close. Used as a location in TV series *Beverly Hills, 90210*, the house is a private residence.

Century City

The modern high-rise district of Century City, just south of Beverly Hills, is best known for one of LA's largest shopping malls, Westfield Century City (www.westfield.com/centurycity; Mon–Sat 10am–9pm, Sun 11am–7pm), but it also harbors a couple of intriguing sights. The **Annenberg Space for Photography** (2000 Avenue of the Stars; www.annenbergspaceforphotography.org; Wed–Sun 11am–6pm; free) exhibits both digital and print photography – the circular digital gallery is especially eye-popping. **The Museum of Tolerance** (9786 W Pico Boulevard, at Roxbury Drive; www.museumoftolerance.com; Mon–Fri & Sun 10am–5pm; Anne exhibit Sun–Wed 10am–6.30pm, Thu 10am–9.30pm, Fri 10am–5pm) is an extraordinary interactive experience charting the story of Fascism and the genocide of the Jews. Multimedia re-enactments outline the rise of Nazism to a harrowing conclusion in a replica gas chamber. The key exhibit (with separate admission), simply entitled 'Anne,' focuses on the life and legacy of Anne Frank through rare artifacts, photographs, and a copy of her original diary.

BEVERLY HILLS HOTEL

From the O'Neill House it's an easy 20-minute walk north along tree-lined, residential Rodeo Drive to Sunset Boulevard and the legendary **Beverly Hills Hotel** ⑩ (9641 Sunset Boulevard; www.dorchestercollection.com). The highly iconic florid pink-plaster palace opened in 1912 to attract wealthy settlers to what was then a town of just 500 people. Since the 1930s it has been a favorite haunt of Hollywood stars and global celebrities, its luxury 'bungalows' serving as temporary homes for the likes of Elizabeth Taylor, Marilyn Monroe, John Lennon, and Donald Trump. Today the hotel is managed by the Dorchester Collection, on behalf of ultimate owner, the Sultan of Brunei. The hotel's social cachet makes its *Polo Lounge* a prime spot for movie execs to power lunch. Grab a coffee or snack in the historic **Fountain Coffee Room** (daily 7am–7pm), with its 1950s-style counter (where rock group Guns N' Roses were signed in 1986), or a cocktail at **Bar Nineteen12** (Tue–Sat 6pm–1am).

GREYSTONE MANSION AND PARK

If you still have time, hop in a taxi at the Beverly Hills Hotel to **Greystone Mansion** ⑪ (905 Loma Vista Drive; www.greystonemansion.org; park daily 10am–5pm; free), around 1.4 miles (2.3km) to the northeast. The biggest house in Beverly Hills, this 50,000-sq-ft (4,645-sq-meter) Tudor-style palace was

built in 1928 by oil titan Edward Doheny (his son, Ned Doheny, was murdered here one year later). It's a favorite movie location, appearing in *There Will Be Blood* (2007), *The Big Lebowski* (1998), and even *Star Trek Into Darkness* (2013), among others. Though rarely open, the mansion does host Friends of Greystone events throughout the year (see website), and the **Music in the Mansion** chamber music program (monthly Sundays Jan–June, 2pm).

The grounds are now maintained as a public park, so you can admire the mansion's limestone facade and intricately designed chimneys for free, then stroll through the 16-acre (6.5 hectare) gardens, where you'll find koi-filled ponds and expansive views of the LA sprawl. If you visit in the winter try to attend one of the special performances of **The Manor** by Katherine Bates and **Theatre 40**; the audience follows the actors through the first floor of Greystone Mansion as the tragedy unfolds (https://theatre40.org). From the park, take a taxi back to downtown Beverly Hills and the end the day with dinner at Wolfgang Puck's fancy **Spago**, see ❸.

The Witch's House

The Spadena House at 516 Walden Drive is better known as The Witch's House, thanks to its Brothers' Grimm fairytale exterior. The house was built by Hollywood art director Harry Oliver in 1921 for Irvin Willat's Culver City studio, and starred in a few movies of the silent era. After the studio closed, the Spadena family moved the home to its current location in 1934 and it appeared (briefly) in 1995 cult movie *Clueless*.

Food and Drink

❶ CHAUMONT BAKERY & CAFÉ

143 S Beverly Drive; tel: 310-550 5510; www.chaumontbakery.com; Mon–Thu 6.30am–6.30pm, Fri & Sat 6.30am–4pm, Sun 7.30am–2pm; $
French-style bakery and café serving wonderful organic breakfasts.

❷ NATE'N AL DELICATESSEN

414 N Beverly Drive; tel: 310-274 0101; https://natenal.com; daily 7am–9pm; $
The best-known Jewish deli in Beverly Hills, here since 1945, famed for its smoked fish, beef hot dogs, and potato pancakes.

❸ SPAGO

176 N Cañon Drive; tel: 310-385 0880; www.wolfgangpuck.com/dining/spago; Mon 6–10pm, Tue–Fri noon–2.30pm & 6–10pm, Sat noon–2.30pm & 5.30–10.30pm, Sun 5.30–10pm; $$$
Flagship restaurant that helped nationalize Californian cuisine, and still good for Wolfgang Puck's latest concoctions.

The Warner Bros. Water Tower

BURBANK STUDIOS

Northwest of Downtown LA, Burbank, not Hollywood, is where the modern movie and media industry has its home. Walt Disney, Warner Bros, and Nickelodeon are all here, with Universal Studios and its massive theme park next door in Universal City.

DISTANCE: 3 miles (4.8km)
TIME: One to two days
START: Warner Bros. Studios
END: Universal CityWalk
POINTS TO NOTE: Metrolink links Downtown LA with Burbank, from where bus No. 155 will get you to Warner Bros; the Universal City station on the Metro Red Line is right next to Universal Studios. Alternatively, driving is fairly straightforward, with plenty of parking at both attractions. With careful planning, in a long day you can hit most of the highlights here. But if you want to catch everything, it's best to allow one full day for Universal. Download the 'Official Universal Studios Hollywood App' for maps, wait times, show times, and access to free Wi-Fi.

Burbank was a small farming community until rapid expansion in the 1950s turned it into a suburb of LA. Movie studios have had a presence here since the 1920s, but many movie and TV studios relocated from Hollywood wholesale in the 1960s and 1970s. NBC completed a lavish new Burbank complex in 1962, while Walt Disney and Warner Bros. ended up nearby in what is now known as the 'Media District.' Just across the Los Angeles River, Universal City is named after Universal Pictures, now home to the Universal Studios Hollywood film studio and theme park, and the Universal CityWalk shopping and entertainment center.

WARNER BROS. STUDIOS

Make an early start at **Warner Bros. Studios ❶** (3400 W Riverside Drive; www.wbstudiotour.com; daily 8.30am–3pm), which offers fascinating 3-hour tours (via carts) of its sizeable facilities and active backlot, where *ER* and *Friends* were filmed in the 1990s, and the Oscar-win-

Live TV show tapings

If you're interesting in watching a live taping of your favorite show, visit www.tvtickets.com for tickets and up-to-date filming schedules.

Warm Warner Bros. welcome   *Universal Studios*

ning movie *La La Land* was put together in 2016. Current TV shows you might see being filmed (you must apply separately for tickets to join audiences) include *The Big Bang Theory*; *Conan* (Conan O'Brien records his TBS talk show from historic Stage 15); *Lucifer*; *Lethal Weapon* (TV series); and the *Ellen Degeneres Show*.

Standard studio tours comprise a two-hour guided portion (taking in an active soundstage and backlot or two, as well as exhibits), plus a self-guided visit to 'Stage 48: Script-to-Screen,' an interactive soundstage exploring key phases of the movie production process. The 'Wizarding World: Harry Potter & Fantastic Beasts Exhibit' features props and costumes from *Fantastic Beasts and Where to Find Them* (2016) and various *Harry Potter* movies, while several batmobiles from the *Batman* movies (1989–2016) are displayed in a special 'batcave.' After visiting the real 'Central Perk' set from the TV show *Friends* on Stage 48, you can grab a coffee or snack from the working Central Perk Café.

UNIVERSAL STUDIOS HOLLYWOOD

Drive or take a taxi to **Universal Studios ❷** (100 Universal City Plaza; www.universal studioshollywood.com; hours vary, check website) in Universal City, 3 miles (4.8km) southwest of Warner Bros. Universal Studios Hollywood is a theme park for everyone who loves movies. Though this is still a working film studio complex, you are unlikely to get

anywhere near filming, but the rides and entertainment are top-class.

WaterWorld

From the entrance gate walk around to **WaterWorld ❸**, the top-rated show at Universal Studios (every 20 minutes). Based on the 1995 post-apocalyptic action movie, expect jumping jet-skiers and crazy stunts, dives, massive fire-fights, and explosions (including giant fireballs rising 50ft/15 meters in the air), and even a simulated plane crash.

Wizarding World of Harry Potter

Continue from WaterWorld, keeping Universal Plaza to your left, to the **Wizarding World of Harry Potter**. Whether you just want to visit the shops of Hogsmeade, enjoy a butterbeer at the **Three Broomsticks & Hog's Head**, see ❶, or are game for a full-on thrill ride, you will feel as if you are part of Harry Potter's world. **Flight of the Hippogrif ❹** is a family-friendly roller coaster that spirals and dives around a pumpkin patch, and then swoops past Hagrid's hut. The **Harry Potter and the Forbidden Journey ❺** motion simulation ride takes you inside Hogwarts, through Dumbledore's office, and the Gryffindor common room.

Studio Tour

Park admission includes the **Studio Tour ❻** (every 5–10 minutes; 1hr) of the historic studio lots behind the theme park. The first half of the tour features a tram ride through a make-believe set where you get up close and personal with the shark from *Jaws*, see the motel from *Psycho*, and experience a high-speed car chase in *Fast & Furious – Supercharged!* You'll also see the Wisteria Lane set from hit series *Desperate Housewives*. Comedian Jimmy Fallon acts as video host of the tour, with video clips on HD monitors in the trams enhancing the commentary.

The Simpsons Ride

Back in the main park, the **Simpsons Ride ❼** is wacky virtual-reality FERRY into the Krustyland theme-park-within-in-a-theme-park; nearby at **Springfield USA ❽** you can eat at Krusty Burger, buy souvenirs at the Kwik-E-Mart, or grab a beer at Moe's Tavern.

The Lower Lot

The escalator down to the **Lower Lot** leads to some seriously entertaining rides, beginning with **Revenge of the Mummy ❾**, a ride through sets inspired by *The Mummy* movies. **Transformers: The Ride-3D ❿** is an immersive, next generation thrill ride blending media and flight simulation technology. Finally, **Jurassic Park: The Ride ⓫** is an exhilarating water ride, a giant log flume with a 84ft (25 meters) plunge at the end.

Special Effects Show

Back in the Upper Lot, the **Special Effects Show ⓬** stars Hollywood's best stunt performers as they demonstrate the secrets behind realistic physical combat sequences, horror scenes, zero-grav-

Universal CityWalk dressed in neon

ity space travel, and even live animation (every 20 minutes).

Universal's Animal Actors
Next door, the **Universal's Animal Actors**  show re-enacts favorite scenes from *The Secret Life of Pets* (2016), plus all sorts of tricks performed by animal stars (20 minutes). For a good lunch or snack stop, head to **Mel's Diner,** see ②, a short stroll from here.

Despicable Me action
Super Silly Funland ⑭ is a colorfully themed, interactive Minion-inspired outdoor venue, a literal interpretation of the seaside carnival from the *Despicable Me* (2010) movie, guaranteed to excite kids of all ages with more than 80 different water-play features.

Next, the **Despicable Me Minion May-**hem ⑮ 3-D motion simulator is where kids start by becoming a minion and going through 'minion-training' before taking a ride through Gru's super-villain laboratory.

The Walking Dead Attraction
Themed on the cult TV show, **The Walking Dead Attraction** ⑯ is a scary walk-through experience, replete with zombies and other post-apocalyptic fun.

UNIVERSAL CITYWALK

This three-block entertainment, dining, and shopping promenade (www.citywalkhollywood.com), is just next door to Universal Studios, with stores and restaurants open to 10pm most evenings. The food is fairly standard chain fare, with **Karl Strauss Brewing Co,** see ③, one of the better options.

Food and Drink

① THREE BROOMSTICKS & HOG'S HEAD
Wizarding World, Universal Studios; tel: 800-864 8377; $$
Rustic tavern inspired by the *Harry Potter* books, featuring British staples plus 'butterbeer' (a butterscotch soft drink, with no alcohol). The Hog's Head is the pub at the back.

② MEL'S DINER
Off Universal Plaza, Universal Studios; tel: 800-864 8377; $$

Classic, American Graffiti-inspired 50s drive-in diner. Expect burgers and fries, chicken fingers, root beer floats, and frosty milkshakes.

③ KARL STRAUSS BREWING CO
1000 Universal Studios Boulevard (Universal CityWalk); tel: 818-753 2739; www.karlstrauss.com; Sun–Thu 11am–9pm, Fri & Sat 11am–11pm; $$
Outpost of the excellent San Diego microbrewery, offering Big Barrel IPA, Red Trolley Ale, and Wreck Alley Imperial Stout on tap, as well as a hearty menu.

DISNEYLAND

Walt Disney's first theme park put Anaheim, just east of LA, on the map, and it remains a global showstopper. All the classic Disneyland rides and characters are here, spread throughout eight different 'lands,' which encircle the towering spires of Sleeping Beauty Castle.

PARK SIZE: 85 acres (34 hectares); expanding to about 100 acres (40 hectares) with Star Wars Land (2019)
TIME: A full day
START/END: Main Street, USA
POINTS TO NOTE: From Downtown LA it takes about 45 mins by car; by train its 30 mins to Fullerton, from where OCTD buses will drop you at Disneyland. Alternatively from Downtown LA, MTA No. 460 takes about 90 mins. Greyhound takes 45 mins from LA to Anaheim bus station.

In the 1940s, illustrator and film maker Walt Disney conceived a theme park where his famous cartoon characters – Mickey Mouse, Donald Duck, Goofy and the rest – would come to life. Since its debut in 1955, **Disneyland** has been one of the defining hallmarks of American culture, an international theme-park phenomenon that's been expanding ever since it opened, with the latest addition, Star Wars: Galaxy's Edge, slated for 2019. Today the whole complex falls under the **Disneyland Resort** umbrella, which includes three hotels and a shopping, dining, and entertainment complex known as **Downtown Disney**.

There's no single best way to tour Disneyland. The route you take will depend on whether you have children (and their ages), love thrill rides, are a first-time visitor, or have more than one day to spend. FastPass times will also determine how you organize your day. Use the Disneyland Mobile App to check wait times for each attraction. The best advice for everyone is to arrive early and head for the attraction you most want to see first.

There is only one entrance, which leads into Main Street, USA. From here, our route proceeds clockwise through the eight other 'lands,' of the park.

MAIN STREET, USA

From the front gates, **Main Street, USA ❶** leads through a scaled-down replica of a bucolic Midwestern town, filled with souvenir shops and diners, toward **Central Plaza ❷**, aka 'the Hub.' At the foot of Main Street as you enter

California's Disneyland is the original, opened in 1955

Town Square is the Disney Gallery and the Opera House. The latter showcases **Great Moments with Mr. Lincoln**, featuring an audio-animatronic version of the beloved 16th president of the USA. If you don't fancy walking, you can traverse Main Street via classic horse-drawn streetcar, omnibus, jitney, or fire truck.

Alternatively, you may want to hop aboard the **Disneyland Railroad** at the entrance for an 18-minute steam-train ride around the park (every 5–10 mins). It's a good way of seeing the various lands, or zipping across to Tomorrowland, New Orleans Square, and Mickey's Toontown.

Sleeping Beauty's Castle

At the center of Disneyland and immediately north of Central Plaza stands **Sleeping Beauty's Castle** ❸, a pseudo-Rhineland palace with narrow corridors and stairs leading to brightly colored 3-D scenes from the classic Disney cartoon. The castle also provides an entrance to Fantasyland.

ADVENTURELAND

Like spokes on a wheel, paths lead out from the Hub (Central Plaza) in front of the castle to each 'land.' Turn left (southwest) and head into **Adventureland**, with rides and attractions themed around 'exotic' jungles and ancient temples (designed to invoke Victorian expeditions to Africa, as well as classic adventure movies).

Jungle Cruise

The tongue-in-cheek **Jungle Cruise** ❹ along a 'tropical' river is an original from 1955. It has 'tour guides' giving corny commentary and crude puns about the fake animatronic beasts creaking amid the scenery. You'll also escape a headhunter or two and sail through a hidden temple. It's 7 minutes of kooky fun.

Indiana Jones Adventure

Next to the Jungle Cruise dock, the **Indiana Jones Adventure** ❺ is a thrill ride in a 12-person troop transportation that realistically simulates driving fast over rough terrain. The ride trundles down skull-encrusted corridors in which you face fireballs, burning rubble, ven-

---

Tickets

There are many ticket options for visiting the Disneyland parks, and taking time to think them through is time – and money – well spent. You can buy a single-day ticket ($97–135) or get tickets for multiple days on a sliding scale. You can then customize your ticket by adding various options: Park Hopper ($185) allows unlimited visits to both Disneyland parks; the Disney MaxPass ($10 extra) allows you to make FastPass selections from your phone; and if you visit for three days or more, a Magic Morning ticket gives one early entry to the park. You can buy tickets at the park entrances, or online at https://disneyland.disney.go.com.

Rags and riches at the Pirates of the Caribbean ride

omous snakes, and, inevitably, a rolling-boulder finale.

NEW ORLEANS SQUARE

Continue walking west to **New Orleans Square**, a lavish recreation of 19th-century New Orleans, complete with French Quarter courtyards, lacy wrought-iron balconies, and jazz bands. This area contains two of the best rides in the park, as well as the tastiest food – try **Blue Bayou**, see ➊.

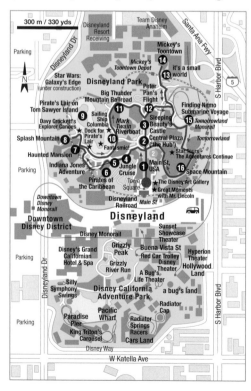

Pirates of the Caribbean
Everyone loves the **Pirates of the Caribbean** ➏, a 15-minute boat ride through underground caverns, and down a small waterfall, singing along with drunken pirates in dungeons, and a burning, looted city.

Haunted Mansion
Head over to the grand Southern-style **Haunted Mansion** ➐, a riotous 'doom buggy' tour in the company of the house spooks and spiritualist Madame Leota.

CRITTER COUNTRY

Just beyond the Haunted Mansion lies **Critter Country**. This area is themed around the great American Northwoods, with towering pines, waterfalls, and suitably rustic buildings. You can ride in a real, 20-person canoe at Davy Crockett's Explorer Canoes, which makes a full circle around Pirate's Lair on Tom Sawyer Island.

The impressive Sailing Ship Columbia

Splash Mountain

Inspired by the animated sequences of the 1946 Disney film *Song of the South*, **Splash Mountain** ❽ starts off innocently enough as you ride a log flume past brightly colored scenes from the movie. Suddenly you emerge at the top of the mountain and plunge down into Brer Rabbit's Laughin' Place with a mighty splash. Those in the front and on the right are sure to get soaked, but it's a great way to cool off on a hot day.

FRONTIERLAND

On the other side of the river from Critter Country lies **Frontierland**, which re-creates rustic settings from America's 19th-century Wild West. As you walk east along the river to the main section, you'll pass the boat dock for Pirate's Lair on Tom Sawyer Island.

Pirate's Lair on Tom Sawyer Island

The **Pirate's Lair on Tom Sawyer Island** ❾ adventure begins with a log raft ride across the river. The island recalls the story of Tom Sawyer and Huck Finn running away to live the carefree lives of pirates. It's a self-guided tour culminating in the unearthing of pirate loot at the Treasure Dig.

Mark Twain Riverboat

Continue into the heart of Frontierland for the **Mark Twain** Riverboat ❿, a 19th-century-inspired Mark Twain paddle steamer that takes a 14-minute spin around the island. The **Sailing Ship Columbia**, a 110ft (33.5-meter) -long, fully rigged replica of the 18th-century frigate that discovered the Columbia River, also makes cruises from here.

Big Thunder Mountain Railroad

More thrills await at **Big Thunder Mountain Railroad** ⓫, just across from the dock. The train cars whip around tight curves, through dark tunnels, and down into canyons beneath the mountain's red rock spires, darting through the ghost town of Big Thunder. Not as terrifying as the big roller coasters, this is a good option for more timid souls.

FANTASYLAND

Continue behind Big Thunder Mountain to reach **Fantasyland**, inspired

---

Beat the lines

On busy days, waits of 1–2 hours are not uncommon for popular attractions. Use Disney's FastPass system to make the most of your time; this allows you to jump the line at certain rides, though daily availability is limited and not guaranteed. Purchasing the Disney MaxPass allows you to make FastPass selections on your phone via the Disneyland app; alternatively, you can use the FastPass distribution points near the entrances of select attractions at the park.

Mickey Mouse flying high

by the fairytale medieval villages of France, Germany, Switzerland, and England: this is where little ones can encounter all their favorite Disney princesses, from Snow White to Sleeping Beauty and Cinderella.

Peter Pan's Flight

Just beneath Sleeping Beauty Castle, **Peter Pan's Flight** ⑫ is an enchanting ride over London by night to Neverland, with all the characters of this timeless tale. However, it has one of the slowest-moving lines in the park and much of the charm of this popu-

lar 3-minute ride is lost after lining up for an hour or more. Get there early, or get a FastPass (see page 63).

'it's a small world'

Lines move more quickly at the northern end of **Fantasyland**, as guests board small boats for a leisurely float around the globe in **it's a small world** ⑬. This whimsical audio-animatronic attraction features dolls from around the world dressed in bright traditional costumes, dancing and singing the catchy theme tune in their own languages.

MICKEY'S TOONTOWN

For tots who just can't get enough of cartoons, there's **Mickey's Toontown** ⑭, just beyond the railroad tracks north of Fantasyland. This section is thick with slow-moving bumper cars and other kiddie amusements; explore the houses of Mickey, Minnie, and other classic Disney characters, take 'Lenny the Cab' in Roger Rabbit's Car Toon Spin, or zip around on 'Gadget's Go Coaster.'

TOMORROWLAND

To the southeast of Fantasyland lies **Tomorrowland**, Disney's vision of the future and testimony to the optimism of the 1960s Space Age, its Googie architecture first realized in 1959. Here you can pick up the **Disneyland Monorail**, which whips around the

---

Disneyland ABCs

Address: 1313 Harbor Boulevard, Anaheim

Disney information: https://disneyland.disney.go.com

General park information: 714-781 4636

Disney vacation packages: 714-520 5060, https://disneyland.disney.go.com/vacation-packages

Hotel reservations: 714-956 6425, https://disneyland.disney.go.com/hotels

Restaurant reservations: 714-781-DINE (714-781 3463), https://disneyland.disney.go.com/dining

Opening hours: Can vary widely according to season, day of the week, and special events. Typical hours are daily 8am–midnight, but always check ahead.

New Orleans–themed Blue Bayou

whole resort (beyond the theme park) in around 13 minutes, stopping at the Downtown Disney District.

Finding Nemo Submarine Voyage

The **Finding Nemo Submarine Voyage** ⓯ gives you a quick underwater tour of the lagoon in a (yellow) research submarine with crystal-clear portholes, where notable aquatic scenes from the hit movie *Finding Nemo* (2003) can be spied.

Space Mountain

Most visitors head straight for **Space Mountain** ⓰, and for many this is a once-in-a-lifetime roller coaster. You ride up a 180ft (55-meter) mountain through the blackness of outer space with only a few twinkling stars, and as your rocket car soars, dives, and whips round tight curves, it feels much faster than its top speed of 28mph (45kph).

Star Tours – The Adventures Continue

One of several *Star Wars* themed attractions in Tomorrowland, **The Adventures Continue** features a flight simulator (doubling as a StarSpeeder 1000) with advanced 3D technology, audio-animatronics characters, and 'in-cockpit' special effects and music.

From Tomorrowland, stroll back down Main Street, USA and find a good spot to take in Disney's **Fantasmic**! (30 mins; 9 & 10.30pm), or the '**Remember...Dreams Come True Fireworks Spectacular**' (select evenings only). Empty bellies should make for the tasty home-cooked buffet at the **Plaza Inn**, see ❷.

California Adventure

The second component of the Disneyland Resort (just south of Disneyland itself) is the **Disney California Adventure Park**, a theme park based on the history and culture of California. Aside from its slightly more exciting roller coasters and better food, the California Adventure is really just another 'land' to visit, albeit a much more expensive one. Visit https://disneyland.disney.go.com/destinations/disney-california-adventure for more details.

Food and Drink

❶ BLUE BAYOU

New Orleans Square; $$$

Upscale Cajun and creole cuisine, with a beautiful outdoor terrace decorated by hanging lanterns.

❷ PLAZA INN

Central Plaza, Main Street, USA; $$

This is one of the originals, a Victorian-themed buffet restaurant said to be a favorite of Walt Disney himself. Expect hearty, American fare.

MIRACLE MILE

Some of the city's greatest museums occupy Miracle Mile, a stretch of Wilshire Boulevard in Central Los Angeles with something for everyone. Admire the art at LACMA and the classic cars at the Petersen Automotive Museum, and explore the prehistoric world at La Brea Tar Pits.

DISTANCE: 0.3 miles (500 meters)
TIME: A full day
START: Petersen Automotive Museum
END: Craft and Folk Art Museum
POINTS TO NOTE: Avoid doing this walk on a Monday (when the Craft and Folk Art Museum is closed) and Wednesday (when LACMA is closed). The easiest way to get here on public transportation is via bus No. 720 from Wilshire/Western metro station (Purple Line). The route is otherwise easy to walk.

The 1.5-mile (2.4km) section of Wilshire between Fairfax and Highland avenues (also known as Mid-Wilshire), Miracle Mile got its name in the late 1930s when it was developed as a high-end commercial strip to rival Downtown LA – designed to serve automobile customers rather than pedestrians.

Wilshire is lined with faded Art Deco monuments, notably the El Rey Theatre, a thriving concert venue built in 1936 with a flashy neon sign, and the May Company Department Store's landmark Streamline Moderne building, completed in 1939 and slated to become the Academy Museum. Beginning in 1965 with the arrival of the Los Angeles County Museum of Art, the strip gradually attracted more galleries and museums, giving it another nickname, Museum Row.

PETERSEN AUTOMOTIVE MUSEUM

Start out at the **Petersen Automotive Museum** ❶ (6060 Wilshire Boulevard, at Fairfax; www.petersen.org; daily 10am–6pm) at the western end of Miracle Mile, and work east. The

The Academy Museum

Los Angeles and Hollywood have been crying out for a decent museum dedicated to the movies and the Oscars for years, and it finally looks like happening; sometime in 2019 the Renzo Piano-designed **Academy Museum** should open next door to LACMA on Wilshire Boulevard. Visit www.oscars.org/museum for the latest.

The Petersen Automotive Museum building resembles the shape of a car

impossible-to-miss building was renovated by Kohn Pedersen Fox in 2015, its exterior wrapped in a mesh of stainless-steel ribbons, lit by glowing red LED lights.

Inside are three floors loaded with all kinds of vehicles, with periodic exhibits on topics like custom cars of the 1950s and 1960s, and 'million-dollar' motors. Visits begin on the third 'History' floor, which takes you on a journey through California's vehicular past, including a gallery dedicated to Hollywood (think the Batmobile and the Pontiac Aztek from *Breaking Bad*). 'Industry' is the theme of the second floor (the Forza Motorsports Racing Experience, a racing car simulator, is also here), while the first floor is dedicated to 'Artistry,' featuring the BMW Art Car collection, with cars adorned by the likes of Alexander Calder, David Hockney, and Robin Rhode.

LACMA

Just across the street from the Automotive Museum, the **Los Angeles County Museum of Art ❷** (LACMA; www.lacma.org; Mon, Tue & Thu 11am–5pm, Fri 11am–8pm, Sat & Sun 10am–7pm) is one of the largest museums west of the Mississippi, and certainly one of LA's best. The seven-building complex contains around 100,000 objects dating from ancient times to the present. The museum contains several places to grab food or a drink, including **C+M (Coffee and Milk)**, see ❶.

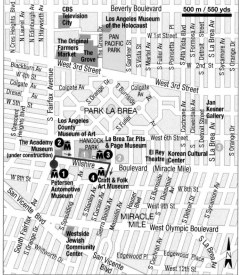

Modern art
The modern art galleries are especially rich in the work of Picasso. His classic Blue Period *Portrait of Sebastia Juñer Vidal* is on show in gallery 225, while his anguished *Weeping Woman with*

La Brea Tar Pits

Handkerchief usually resides in gallery 234. Don't miss *La Gerbe* in the entrance lobby, a huge ceramic installation by Matisse, commissioned for an LA couple in the 1950s and later transported here.

Multicultural highlights

The Miracle Mile is close to a couple of LA's more intriguing cultural enclaves. The **Little Ethiopia** district begins a half-mile (800 meters) south of the Petersen Automotive Museum, with the stretch of Fairfax Avenue between Olympic Boulevard and Whitworth Drive home to numerous Ethiopian restaurants, stores, and businesses. From the Craft and Folk Art Museum it's another half-mile (800-meter) stroll east along Wilshire to the Korean Cultural Center (5505 Wilshire Boulevard; www.kccla.org; Mon–Fri 10am–5pm, Sat 10am–1pm; free), which displays photographs, antiques, and craftwork from Korea and the local Koreatown community. **Koreatown** proper begins another 2.5 miles (4km) east along Wilshire. Just under a mile (1.6km) north of the Petersen Museum, The Grove is home to **LA Farmers' Market** (6333 W 3rd Street, at Fairfax; www.farmersmarketla.com; Mon–Fri 9am–9pm, Sat 9am–8pm, Sun 10am–7pm), a rabbit warren of restaurants, bakeries, and multicultural food stands.

Pavilion for Japanese Art

At the eastern end of the complex, iconoclastic architect Bruce Goff created the exquisite **Pavilion for Japanese Art** to re-create the effects of traditional shoji screens, filtering varying levels and qualities of light through to the interior. Displays include painted screens and scrolls, ceramics, and lacquerware, viewable on a ramp spiraling down to a small, first-floor waterfall that trickles pleasantly amid the near-silence of the gallery.

Art of the Americas

On the south side of the complex, the **Art of the Americas Building** is home to the wonderful Art of the Ancient Americas galleries on Level 4; Jorge Pardo's controversial design for this section is a cross between a cave and hip lounge bar, with display cases that undulate and swell out from the walls in a vivid tangerine color.

LA BREA TAR PITS & MUSEUM

Just next door to LACMA, Hancock Park contains **La Brea Tar Pits** ❸ (www.tarpits.org; daily 6am–10pm; free), LA's most famous natural formations. Comprising the larger Lake Pit and scores of smaller pools of smelly, viscous asphalt (it's not technically tar), the pits date back to the last Ice Age. Primeval creatures from tapirs to mammoths tried to drink from the thin layer of water covering the petroleum in the pits, only to

'Borderlandia: Cultural Top' exhibit at the Craft & Folk Art Museum

become stuck fast and preserved for modern science.

Millions of bones belonging to the animals (and one set of human bones) have been found here since 1913. Some of them are displayed in the on-site **Page Museum** (daily 9.30am–5pm), where you can see skeletons of extinct creatures from giant ground sloths to menacing saber-toothed tigers. Films in the 3-D Theater (extra charge) bring the site to life, and Excavator Tours (included) take you around the whole park and into the Observation Pit and Project 23 dig site on the west side (otherwise off-limits). The park itself is free to wander.

CRAFT & FOLK ART MUSEUM

Cross Wilshire from La Brea Tar Pits to the small but absorbing **Craft & Folk Art Museum** ❹ (www.cafam.org; Tue–Fri 11am–5pm, Sat & Sun 11am–6pm). The carefully curated exhibits include handmade objects from all over the world – rugs, pottery, clothing, and so on – with rotating exhibitions featuring the likes of handmade tarot cards, ceramic folk art, and highly detailed Asian textiles. From here it's a short walk back across the street for dinner at **Callender's Grill**, see ❷, or a 20-minute (1 mile/1.6km) hike farther along Wilshire and up La Brea Avenue for **Republique**, see ❸, one of the city's best restaurants.

Food and Drink

❶ **C+M (COFFEE AND MILK)**

5905 Wilshire Boulevard; tel: 323-857 4761; www.patinagroup.com/cm-lacma; Mon, Tue & Thu 9am–5pm, Fri 9am–7pm, Sat & Sun 9am–6pm; $
Stylish modern coffee shop inside LACMA, offering pastries, cakes, and fresh fruit.

❷ **CALLENDER'S GRILL**

5773 Wilshire Boulevard; tel: 323-937 7952; www.mariecallendersgrill.com; Mon, Tue & Thu 9am–5pm, Fri 9am–7pm, Sat & Sun 9am–6pm; $$
Classic American food in an old-fashioned, Victorian-themed dining room. The menu

includes wood-fired pizzas, meatloaf, chicken pot pie, and pot roast.

❸ **REPUBLIQUE**

624 S La Brea Avenue; tel: 310-362 6115; www.republiquela.com; Sun–Wed 8am–3pm & 5.30–10pm, Thu–Sat 8am–3pm, 5.30–11pm;
$$
Modern French cuisine (with American and Asian influences) from chefs Margarita and Walter Manzke, with dinner served on wooden, communal tables and a bakery providing coffee, pastries, and bread in the mornings. Dishes might include Dover sole a la meuniere, Sonoma duck breast, or Cook Ranch pig's feet.

Playing chess, Chinatown

EL PUEBLO AND CHINATOWN

Explore the Spanish and Mexican origins of Los Angeles, a legacy preserved at the museums, galleries, restaurants, and taco shops of the historic Pueblo section of Downtown. LA's Chinatown also has a long history, with an equally enticing array of markets, noodle shops, and bakeries.

DISTANCE: 1.5 miles (2.4km)
TIME: A full day
START: La Plaza, El Pueblo
END: Thien Hau Temple, Chinatown
POINTS TO NOTE: Avoid doing this walk on a Monday or Tuesday, as most of the museums and galleries close one of those days. El Pueblo is easily accessible by Metro or bus to Union Station; Chinatown has its own Metro station (Gold line) at College and Spring streets.

El Pueblo de Los Angeles, the historic section of Downtown just north of the Financial District, dates back to the foundation of the city in 1781. Over the years decline crept in, and by the 1920s the area was derelict and crime-ridden. Local activist Christine Sterling was instrumental in preserving what was left of Mexican El Pueblo, and Olvera Street, remodelled as a Mexican-style market place, opened in 1930.

From the 1860s, LA's Chinatown grew up in and around El Pueblo, though the community was forced to move in the 1930s to make way for Union Station; what is now Chinatown was formally established in 1938 along North Broadway and North Spring Street. New Chinatown flourished in the 1940s as a tourist attraction, with the main Central Plaza built by Hollywood set designers in a stereotypical, over-the-top Chinese style. Today it remains a vibrant but relatively low-key community, with markets, stores, and restaurants the biggest attractions.

LA PLAZA

Start at **Los Angeles Plaza Park ❶** (or just 'the Plaza'), at the heart of El Pueblo. The site of the historic Spanish settlement of 1818, this is where LA's Hispanic origins are most obvious. Peek inside the old church on the western side, Nuestra Señora Reina de los Angeles or simply **La Placita** (daily 6.30am–8pm). Completed in 1823, this is LA's oldest place of worship.

On the south side of the plaza, the **Old Plaza Firehouse Museum ❷** (Tue–Sun 10am–3pm; free) building dates back to 1884 and contains a small but

The Chinese American Museum

fascinating roomful of fire-fighting gear. Next door, stately **Pico House** was a grand Italianate-style hotel completed in 1870 by Pío Pico, the last governor of California under Mexican rule.

La Plaza de Cultura y Artes

Stroll across to the enlightening **La Plaza de Cultura y Artes ❸** (www.lapca.org; Mon, Wed & Thu noon–5pm, Fri–Sun noon–6pm; free) at the southwest corner of Los Angeles Plaza Park. The main exhibition charts Mexican-American history, beginning with the founding of LA in 1781, with a no-holds-barred review of atrocities committed by the Spanish against the indigenous Tongva. The modern Chicano movement has its own gallery, Calle Principal is an evocative re-creation of Los Angeles Main Street in the 1920s, and temporary exhibits take up the rest of the space.

Chinese American Museum

Walk along the southern edge of La Plaza and turn right on cobblestoned Sanchez Street for the **Chinese American Museum ❹** (www.camla.org; Tue–Sun 10am–3pm;

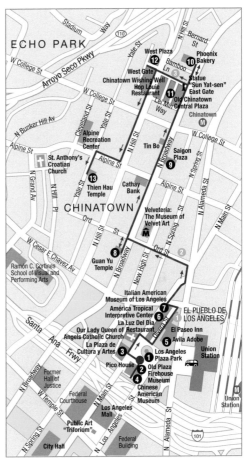

Bustling Olvera Street

free). Housed in the 1890 Garnier Building, the museum chronicles the history of Chinese settlement, society, and culture in this area. Permanent exhibits chart the rise of Chinese communities in LA, immigration from China, and re-create the Sun Wing Wo Chinese herb shop circa 1900.

OLVERA STREET

Running north from Los Angeles Plaza Park, traffic-free **Olvera Street** is Christine Sterling's pseudo-Mexican village market, comprising about 30 old-looking buildings that opened back in 1930. Taken over for numerous festivals throughout the year, the street is at its best on such communal occasions, and regularly features strolling mariachi bands, Aztec- and Mexican-themed processions, and various dancers and artisans. It's also the best place for lunch or a snack; sit down restaurants La Luz Del Dia and El Paseo Inn are excellent, but it's hard to resist the humble taco stand **Cielito Lindo**, see ①, for atmosphere.

Avila Adobe

Christine Sterling's renewal efforts began in the 1920s at the **Avila Adobe** ⑤ (10 Olvera Street; daily 9am–4pm; free). This handsome Spanish colonial-style home is touted as the oldest structure in Los Angeles (c.1818), although it was almost entirely rebuilt out of reinforced concrete following the 1971 Sylmar earthquake. The house is furnished as it might have appeared in the late 1840s, and the courtyard outside contains exhibits on the history of LA's water supply and aspects of *Californio* history, plus a display on Christine Sterling herself.

América Tropical Interpretive Center

David Siqueiros (1896–1974), one of the greatest Mexican artists of the 20th century, painted the epic 80-by-18-ft (24.4-by-5.5 meter) *América Tropical* on the exterior of Italian Hall in El Pueblo in 1932. The mural depicts a Mexican Indian, crucified on a double cross beneath an American eagle – controversial to say the least, it was painted over within a decade. After a mammoth restoration project, what's left of the mural (mostly a ghostly outline) can be seen from a rooftop viewing platform, accessible from the **América Tropical Interpretive Center** ⑥ (https://theamericatropical.org; Tue–Sun 10am–3pm; free). The center provides context about the life, work, and legacy of Siqueiros, with exhibits that examine the mural as a political statement, and its influence on mural artists based in Los Angeles.

Italian American Museum of Los Angeles

Once you reach the northern end of Olvera Street, turn left and left again to round the corner to the **Italian**

Quaint Avila Adobe

The Norton Simon Museum

American Museum of Los Angeles ❼ (103 Main Street; www.italian-hall.org; Tue–Sun 10am–3pm; free). Opened in 2016 in Italian Hall, the museum showcases the contribution of Italian Americans to LA. Little Italy was located in the blocks north of Los Angeles Plaza Park in the early 20th century; it's now Chinatown, your next destination. To get there, walk one block north on Main Street to Alameda and on to the junction with Ord Street. On the corner stands an LA classic, **Philippe the Original French Dip**, see ❷. Walk west on Ord Street to North Broadway from here, and you enter modern Chinatown.

CHINATOWN

LA's **Chinatown** isn't quite the bustling affair you'll find in a number of other US cities, but the main drag, North Broadway, is fascinating to wander. A short walk south of Ord Street, at 649 N Broadway, a traditional Chinese gate gives way to the **Guan Yu Temple** ❽, dedicated to the popular Taoist god Guandi. Walk back up Broadway (heading north), taking in the various gift shops, malls, and markets along the way. Check out the **Cathay Bank** building at No. 777, blending Modern and Chinese styles, and **Tin Bo** at No. 841, one of the oldest traditional Chinese Medicine and herb shops in the city. One of the most atmospheric spots to explore is **Saigon Plaza** ❾, a warren of market stands at 828 N Broadway. Keep walking north to the **Phoenix Bakery** ❿ (969 N Broadway; www.phoenix bakeryinc.com; daily 9am–7.30pm). Chinatown's oldest bakery has been

Detour to Pasadena

From Chinatown the Gold metro line runs nine miles (14.5km) north to Pasadena, a satellite city of LA and the home of Caltech, with enough attractions to fill another full day. Other than wandering the stores and restaurants of Old Pasadena, highlights include the **USC Pacific Asia Museum** (www.pacificasiamuseum.org; Wed–Sun 10am–6pm), a faux-Chinese palace containing thousands of historical treasures and everyday objects from Asia and the Pacific islands; and the excellent **Norton Simon Museum** (www.nortonsimon.org; Mon, Wed & Thu noon–5pm, Fri & Sat 11am–8pm, Sun 11am–5pm), containing the finest collection of Western European paintings in the state. Three miles (4.8km) southeast of Old Pasadena, the fantastic **Huntington Library** (www.huntington.org; Mon & Wed–Sun 10.30am–4.30pm) contains the art collections of Henry Huntington, former owner of the Pacific Electric Railway Company. The Library contains the finest collection of British portraits outside of the UK, including Gainsborough's famous *Blue Boy*.

Philippe The Original

knocking out its famous strawberry whipped-cream cake since 1938, amongst numerous other sweet treats.

OLD CHINATOWN CENTRAL PLAZA

Pedestrian-only **Old Chinatown Central Plaza** ⓫ at 943 N Broadway (just before Phoenix Bakery), was where 'New' Chinatown began in 1938, its faux-Chinese architecture and stores selling an assortment of lanterns, teapots, and jade jewelry making for an enjoyable wander. Enter at the traditional **East Gate** on Broadway, where there's a statue of revered Chinese leader Sun Yat-sen. From here Gin Ling Way cuts through the mall to the **West Gate** on Hill Street, passing the iconic five-tiered pagoda of **Hop Louie Restaurant** (on Mei Ling Way), built in 1941

(the restaurants is now closed). You'll also see the **Wishing Well**, its fanciful grotto based on the Seven Star Cave in China. A good place to eat is **Blossom Vietnamese Restaurant**, see ③.

Cross Hill Street and walk into the similarly traffic-free **West Plaza** ⓬ (aka Chung King Court), added in 1948 and now home to several contemporary **art galleries**.

Thien Hau Temple

It's a half-mile (800 meters) south to **Thien Hau Temple** ⓭, at 756 Yale Street (walk south on Hill Street, make a right at Alpine Street, then left on Yale). One of the district's most traditional Taoist shrines, this one is dedicated to Mazu, the goddess of the sea – it was actually built for Chinese-Vietnamese refugees in 2005.

Food and Drink

① CIELITO LINDO

23 Olvera Street; tel: 213-687 4391; www.cielitolindo.org; Sun–Thu 9am–11pm, Fri & Sat 9am–midnight; $

Celebrated Mexican taco joint at the north end of Olvera since 1934; expect long lines for their tasty fried *taquitos* with shredded beef and avocado sauce.

② PHILIPPE THE ORIGINAL

1001 N Alameda Street; tel: 213-628 3781; www.philippes.com; daily 6am–10pm; $

This 1908 sawdust café serves up the eponymous sandwich with turkey, ham, lamb, pork, or beef dipped in roasting-pan juices. Cash only.

③ BLOSSOM VIETNAMESE RESTAURANT

451 Gin Ling Way; tel: 213-626 8345; www.blossomrestaurant.com; Tue–Sun noon–4pm & 5.30–9pm; $$

Modern Vietnamese set in a rustic-chic space in the heart of Chinatown Central Plaza, specializing in *pho* (soup noodles), noodle salads, and various rice dishes.

Exploring Little Tokyo

LITTLE TOKYO AND THE ARTS DISTRICT

The most vibrant cultural enclave in Downtown LA, Little Tokyo is also home to the dynamic Geffen Contemporary. Farther east, the Arts District is a burgeoning new area of galleries and restaurants occupying former warehouses and abandoned lots.

DISTANCE: 2.7 miles (4.3km)
TIME: A half-day to full day
START: Little Tokyo Visitor Center
END: The Institute of Contemporary Art
POINTS TO NOTE: Avoid doing this walk on a Monday or Tuesday, as most of the museums and galleries close on either of these days. The Little Tokyo/Arts District Station on the Metro Gold line is close to the start of the route, but DASH buses from Downtown also serve the area. You can complete the whole route easily on foot, though the last section may require a taxi. The Little Tokyo and Arts District sections of the route can be broken into two half-day walks, or completed together in one day.

A significant Japanese community has existed in Los Angeles since 1903, flourishing despite the mass internment of Japanese-Americans during World War II. Since the 1970s, new shopping malls and plazas have replaced most of the original buildings, but Little Tokyo has remained an important hub for the Japanese-American community. Today the colorful shopping and restaurant district is centered on historic 1st Street, between San Pedro and Central streets. Just to the east, the Arts District is a once gritty industrial area, where art galleries and restaurants have replaced the factories and warehouses.

LITTLE TOKYO

Begin at the **Little Tokyo Visitor Center ❶** (307 E 1st Street; Mon–Sat 10am–6pm; tel: 213-613 1911, https://littletokyola.org), which provides maps and information. The stores on this row are mostly Japanese originals, including the **Fugetsu-Do Bakery Shop** (www.fugetsu-do.com) at No. 315, maker of Japanese cakes and candy since 1903, and Daikokuya at No. 327, credited with sparking the ramen craze in LA (see page 119).

On the other side of East 1st Street lies the entrance to **Japanese Village Plaza ❷** (most stores daily 9am–6pm; www.japanesevillageplaza.net), marked with the traditional 55ft (17-meter), red-painted **Japanese Village Plaza Fire**

Tower (aka Yagura Tower). Wander south through the pedestrian-only mall, taking in the sushi bars and stores. One of the best eateries is **Mitsuru Cafe**, see ①.

Japanese American Cultural & Community Center

Cross East 2nd Street and keep walking south on Azusa Street, passing through the small plaza on to the serene **James Irvine Japanese Garden** (Tue–Fri 10am–5pm; free). With a 170ft (52-meter) stream running along its sloping hillside, you'll feel a world away from LA's asphalt and concrete. The building next door is the modest **Japanese American Cultural & Community Center** ③ (244 S San Pedro Street; www.jaccc. org), which runs various visual and cul-

---

Skid Row

The area of Downtown Los Angeles known as **Skid Row** – roughly east of Main Street, south of 3rd Street, and west of Alameda Street – has been home to one of the largest populations of homeless people in the US since the late 1930s, with up to 6,000 sleeping rough or in shelters here. The area can be dangerous, but if you'd like to volunteer or make a donation, contact the **Union Rescue Mission** (tel: 888-778 4392; https://urm.org), **Midnight Mission** (www.midnightmission.org), or the **Downtown Women's Center** (www. downtownwomenscenter.org).

---

tural art programs throughout the year at the adjacent Aratani Theatre. Its Doizaki Gallery (Tue–Fri noon–5pm, Sat & Sun 11am–4pm; free) displays traditional and contemporary Japanese drawing and calligraphy, along with costumes, sculptures, and other art forms.

Higashi Honganji Buddhist Temple

Continue along South San Pedro Street to East 3rd Street and turn left (east). At the corner of South Central Avenue lies the grand **Higashi Honganji Buddhist Temple** ④ (daily 10am–5pm), founded in 1904. The current highly authentic incarnation was completed here in 1976.

Japanese American National Museum

Walk two blocks north along South Central Avenue to the lavish modern premises of the **Japanese American National Museum** ⑤ (100 N Central Avenue; www.janm.org; Tue, Wed, & Fri–Sun 11am–5pm, Thu noon–8pm). This exhibits everything from origami to traditional furniture. Opposite, the **Go For Broke National Education Center** (www.goforbroke.org; Tue, Wed, & Fri 11am–6pm, Thu noon–8pm, Sat 10am–6pm, Sun 11am–6pm) contains the 'Defining Courage Experience,' with hands-on exhibits charting the challenging experiences of Japanese Americans in World War II.

The Geffen Contemporary at MOCA

Just to the north of the Japanese Museum lies the **Geffen Contemporary**

Mike Kelley exhibit at the Geffen Contemporary at MOCA

at MOCA ❻ (www.moca.org; Mon, Wed, & Fri 11am–6pm, Thu 11am–8pm, Sat & Sun 11am–5pm). Built in 1947 for Union Hardware and later used as a police garage, the space was artfully renovated by Frank Gehry in the 1980s and is now the alternative gallery to its more mainstream sibling, the Museum of Contemporary Art (see page 35). It's a massive hall with huge installation pieces, architecture retrospectives, and other big shows with a voracious need for space.

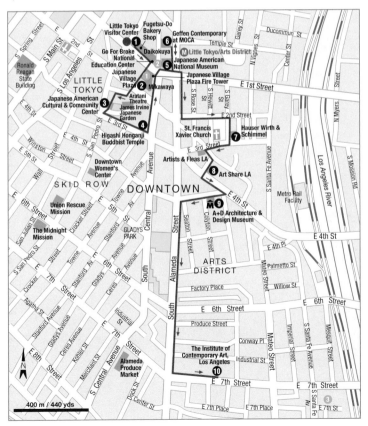

'More Love Hours Than Can Ever Be Repaid' exhibit at the Geffen Contemporary at MOCA

THE ARTS DISTRICT

Walk south on Alameda Street to reach the up-and-coming **Arts District**, which officially begins south of East 1st Street – if you need a break on the way, stop at the **Chado Tea House** (at the Japanese American National Museum), see ②.

Make a left on East 2nd Street and walk east to South Garey Street; one block south along here **Hauser Wirth & Schimmel** ❼ (www.hauserwirth.com; Wed & Fri–Sun 11am–6pm, Thu 11am–8pm), at 901 E 3rd Street, is one of the area's most high-profile galleries. Walk west on East 3rd to the intersection with Traction Avenue and **Artists & Fleas LA** (www.artistsandfleas.com; usual hours Sat 11am–5pm), an arts and crafts market. Stroll south on Traction and right on Hewitt Street to reach **Art Share LA** ❽ (801 E 4th Place; https://artsharela.org; Wed–Sun 1–6pm), which provides subsidized work lofts for artists and runs its own gal-

lery. A short walk south on East 4th Place then right on East 4th, budding architects will enjoy the **A+D Architecture & Design Museum** ❾ (900 E 4th Street; www.aplusd.org; Tue–Fri 11am–5pm, Sat & Sun noon–6pm), which puts on rotating exhibits that feature especially progressive architecture and design.

The Institute of Contemporary Art

From here it's a 20-minute (1 mile/1.6km) walk to The **Institute of Contemporary Art, Los Angeles** ❿ (1717 E 7th Street; www.theicala.org; Wed–Fri 11am–7pm, Sat & Sun 11am–6pm); take a taxi or walk west along East 4th to Alameda and turn left (south), turning left again when you reach East 7th Street. The Institute has a massive exhibition space, allowing for some giant, very creative installations and exhibitions (which rotate).

End the evening with drinks or a meal at fashionable **Bestia**, see ③, 10 minute-walk east along East 7th Street.

Food and Drink

❶ MITSURU CAFE
117 Japanese Village Plaza; tel: 213-613 1028; Tue–Sat 11am–9pm, Sun 11am–7pm; $
Authentic Japanese street snacks including ice cream sandwiches and mochi balls.

❷ CHADO TEA ROOM
369 E 1st Street (Japanese American National Museum); tel: 213-258 2531; www.chadotea.com; daily 11am–6pm; $
Refined café specializing in fine teas and afternoon snacks.

❸ BESTIA
2121 E 7th Place; tel: 213-514 5724; www.bestiala.com; Mon–Thu 5–11pm, Fri & Sat 5pm–midnight; $$
Happening bar and modern Italian restaurant from Ori Menashe and Genevieve Gergis.

University of Southern California

USC AND EXPOSITION PARK

South of Downtown LA, the beautiful campus of the University of Southern California (USC), along with neighboring Exposition Park, offers a heavy dose of culture, thanks to renowned institutions such as the Fisher Museum of Art.

DISTANCE: 2 miles (3.2km)
TIME: A full day
START/END: Expo Park/USC Station (Metro Expo Line)

Founded in 1880, USC is one of the most expensive universities in the country. For visitors, the main attraction is its University Park campus, largely traffic-free and studded with landscaped gardens and handsome 1920s Romanesque Revival-style buildings. Across Exposition Boulevard from the USC campus, 160-acre (65-hectare) Exposition Park incorporates lush manicured gardens and a number of enticing museums that kids will love.

UNIVERSITY OF SOUTHERN CALIFORNIA

Exit the Expo Park/USC metro station at the platform's western end and walk north into the USC campus (http://visit.usc.edu/tours). Immediately on your left is the **Mudd Hall of Philosophy ❶** and

its 146ft (44.5-meter) clock tower, one of USC's most beautiful buildings. Continue walking north on Trousdale Parkway, the main campus thoroughfare, up to the wide expanse of Alumni Park. To the left (west) side of the park is the stately Bovard Administration Building (1921), and its iconic central tower. Look for the bronze statue known as 'Tommy Trojan' beneath it – installed in 1930 to commemorate USC's 50th anniversary. On the other side of the park stands the **Doheny Memorial Library ❷** (1932), nine floors stacked with approximately 790,000 books. Go inside to admire its bronze doors, marble rotunda, stained-glass windows depicting six of the world's great scholars, and the Roman travertine floors and stairway. Grab a drink or a snack in the library café, **LiteraTea**, see ❶.

Head back across Alumni Park and walk northwest into Founders Park. At the park's northwest corner is the Eileen Norris Cinema Theatre, where the **Frank Sinatra Hall ❸** commemorates the legendary singer and actor's life with extensive memorabilia. From here it's a short stroll west to the **Hugh**

Natural History Museum dinosaur skeleton

M. Hefner Hall ❹ (Hefner was another USC donor), which features rotating exhibits of classic Hollywood memorabilia. From here walk south on Watt Way, turning left just before you reach Exposition Boulevard for the Fisher Museum of Art.

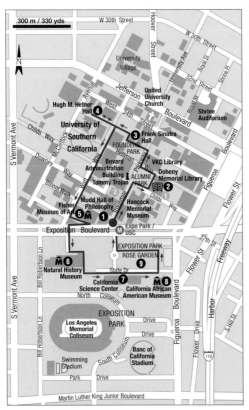

Fisher Museum of Art

The **Fisher Museum of Art ❺** (823 Exposition Boulevard; http://fisher.usc.edu; Tue–Fri noon–5pm, Sat noon–4pm; free), founded in 1939 by oil heiress and collector Elizabeth Holmes Fisher, houses USC's art collection. At least one exhibition a year features art from the encyclopedic permanent collection (dating from 1500 to the present day), with gems such as *Venus Wounded by a Thorn* by Rubens. Before leaving campus, grab lunch at **Moreton Fig**, see ❷.

EXPOSITION PARK

Natural History Museum

To enter Exposition Park, cross Exposition Boulevard at Watt Way and go straight into the **Natural History Museum ❻** (https://nhm.org; daily 9.30am–5pm), always a big hit with kids. Foremost among the exhibits is the Dinosaur Hall, containing a tremendous stash of dinosaur bones and fossils, including a range of Tyrannosaurus Rex specimens. More contemporary bones of Ice Age-era beasts are also on view –

Suspended aircraft at the California Science Center

many of them dug out of the muck of the La Brea Tar Pits (see page 68).

In the fascinating California History Hall, the development of LA is charted with a series of dioramas from the 1930s and Walt Disney's animation stand from 1923. Topping the whole place off is the Hall of Gems and Minerals, several astonishing roomfuls of crystals and a gold display. The Butterfly Pavilion (mid-Apr–early Oct) and Spider Pavilion (mid-Sept–early Nov) require timed tickets.

California Science Center

One of the highlights of Exposition Park is the **California Science Center** ❼ (https://californiasciencecenter.org; daily 10am–5pm; free) next door, with scores of quirky displays making the world of science fun for youngsters. In 2012 it also became the final home of the Space Shuttle *Endeavour* and an excellent accompanying exhibition (timed tickets required on weekends and holidays; free). Other displays include a real A-12 Blackbird spy plane, a walk-in periscope, and an imitation earthquake. The center's IMAX plays kid-oriented documentaries.

California African American Museum

Just to the east of the Science Center, the **California African American Museum** ❽ (https://caamuseum.org; Tue–Sat 10am–5pm, Sun 11am–5pm) contains diverse temporary exhibitions on African American history and culture (with special emphasis on California), as well as a good range of painting and sculpture from African American and African artists. Head back to Expo Park/USC Station by strolling northwest through the **Exposition Park Rose Garden** ❾ (daily 9am–sunset; closed Jan–mid-March), a beautiful oasis at its blooming best April through November.

The USC Trojans

Just south of USC and Exposition Park, the **Los Angeles Memorial Coliseum** was the site of the 1932 and 1984 Olympic Games (and will host them again in 2028). Today it's home to the dominant USC (American) football team, the Trojans. If you can't make a game, take one of the **Los Angeles Coliseum Historic Tours** (1hr 30 mins; tel: 213-741 0410; usually Wed–Sun 10am–1.30pm).

Food and Drink

❶ LITERATEA

3550 Trousdale Parkway; tel: 213-821 4261; http://hospitality.usc.edu/dining_locations/literatea; Mon–Fri 7.30am–2pm; $
Artsy teahouse offering top-notch snacks.

❷ MORETON FIG

3607 Trousdale Parkway; tel: 213-821 3441; www.moretonfig.com; Mon–Fri 11am–3pm & 3.30–8pm; $$$
USC campus restaurant with a focus on farm-to-table Californian cuisine.

GRIFFITH PARK

The Griffith Observatory stands as one of LA's most famous landmarks, high above the city in a park crammed with family-friendly attractions, from miniature trains and a zoo to old-fashioned carousels and wild hiking trails through the Santa Monica Mountains.

DISTANCE: 12 miles (19km)
TIME: A full day
START: Ferndell
END: Forest Lawn Hollywood Hills
POINTS TO NOTE: This is a great route for families. Although Sunday is the best day to see everything, the park gets extremely crowded on weekends – try to visit Tuesday to Friday. The two sections of the route are designed to be completed by car. The park is free and opens daily 5am–10.30pm, though mountain roads close at dusk (www.laparks.org/griffithpark).

Built on land donated by Gilded Age mining millionaire Griffith J. Griffith in 1896, vast Griffith Park, between Los Feliz and the San Fernando Valley, offers gentle greenery and rugged mountain slopes, a welcome respite from the chaos of LA. The only thing marring the landscape is the occasional wildfire – be alert if you arrive at the height of summer.

There are two main park entrances. The start of this route is Western Canyon Road, north of Los Feliz Boulevard, which enters the park through Ferndell – as the name suggests, a lush glade of ferns, from which numerous trails run deeper into the park – and continues up to the Griffith Observatory. The route exits at the northern end of the park, over the hills in the San Fernando Valley, easily accessible from the Ventura Freeway. The tour divides into two distinct sections.

GRIFFITH OBSERVATORY

Begin the route on **Ferndell ❶**, off Los Feliz Boulevard, the leafy southern section of Griffith Park. A half mile (800 meters) along the road, **The Trails Café**, see ❶, is a good spot for breakfast. There are also several easy hiking trails around here – if you have the energy, the short (1 mile/1.6km) but steep hike up to the **Griffith Observatory ❷** (www.griffithobservatory.org; Tue–Fri noon–10pm, Sat & Sun 10am–10pm) will save you parking at the top, which can be overcrowded. Otherwise the drive up is just over 2 miles (3.2km) – you could also detour on the way to take a look

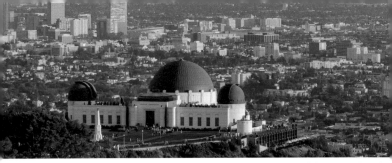

Griffith Observatory and the cityscape beyond

at the **Greek Theatre** ❸ (www.lagreek theatre.com), an open-air amphitheater completed in 1930.

The Observatory itself was completed as a WPA (Works Progress Administration) project in 1935, familiar today from its use as a backdrop in *Rebel Without a Cause*, *Charlie's Angels: Full Throttle*, *Transformers*, and numerous low-budget sci-fi flicks. This astronomical icon now presents an array of high-tech exhibits for young and old alike – highlighted by the 12ins (305mm) Zeiss refracting telescope, the trio of solar telescopes for viewing sunspots and solar storms, and other assorted, smaller telescopes set up on selected evenings for inspecting the firmament at your own pace. Modern displays cover the history of astronomy and human observation, including a 150ft (46-meter) timeline of the universe. The attached **Samuel Oschin Planetarium** shows four different movies. Before you leave, grab a snack at the **Café at the End of the Universe**, see ❷.

GRIFFITH PARK NORTH

From Griffith Observatory, the direct way to reach the northern sector of the park is a winding 2- to 3-hour hike. By car it's a relatively simple 5-mile (8km) detour down the mountain on Vermont Canyon Road/Vermont Avenue (past the Greek Theatre), east on Los Feliz Boulevard, then north on Crystal Springs Drive. This section is a bonanza for families, with attractions beginning with the **Griffith Park & Southern Railroad** ❹ (4400 Crystal Springs Drive; www.griffithpark trainrides.com; daily 10am–4pm). Miniature trains have operated here since the late 1940s, with the current mile (1.6km) of track serviced by one-third scale reproductions of classic Ameri-

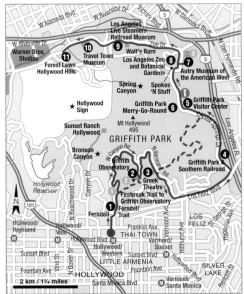

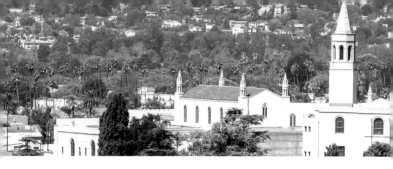

can trains of the 20th century. Around 1.2 miles (1.9km) north of here, the park rangers at **Griffith Park Visitor Center** ⑤ (daily 6.45am–11pm) can provide updates on events and activities in the park, including the nearby **Griffith Park Merry-Go-Round** ⑥ (Sat–Sun 11am–5pm, daily July & Aug). Built in 1926 and brought to the park in 1937, this old-fashioned carousel features 68 finely carved, jumping horses, accompanied by band-organ march and waltz music.

Autry Museum of the American West

Some 1.5 miles (2.4km) north of the visitor center on Crystal Springs Drive,

the **Autry Museum of the American West** ⑦ (https://theautry.org; Tue–Fri 10am–4pm, Sat & Sun 10am–5pm) was founded in 1988 by Gene Autry, the 'singing cowboy.' Autry cut more than 600 discs beginning in 1929, starred in blockbuster Hollywood Westerns during the 1930s and 1940s, and became even more of a household name through his TV show in the 1950s. His permanent collection of Americana – from tribal clothing and religious figurines to Albert Bierstadt paintings and Frederic Remington's romantic sculptures of early 20th-century Western life – offers an insight into the many cultures that have shaped the West. Autry's **Crossroads West Café**, see ③, makes a convenient pit-stop.

Los Angeles Zoo

Opposite the Autry, kids will enjoy the **Los Angeles Zoo and Botanical Gardens** ⑧ (www.lazoo.org; daily 10am–5pm), one of the biggest zoos in the country and home to over 1,000 creatures.

Miniature railroads

Several family-friendly train-related attractions lie farther west along Zoo Drive, beginning with the Sunday-only **Los Angeles Live Steamers Railroad Museum** ⑨ (www.lals.org; Sun 11am–3pm), which operates 7.5-ins (19cm) gauge model trains. Also part of the museum is **Walt's Barn**, a quaint red barn built by Walt Disney in the 1950s as a replica of his child-

---

Los Feliz, Thai Town, & Little Armenia

The neighborhood immediately south of Griffith Park is **Los Feliz**, an affluent, hillside district crammed with expensive mansions and celebrity inhabitants – you'll find some excellent restaurants and stores on Hillhurst Avenue. **Thai Town** runs along Hollywood Boulevard between Normandie and Western, just a half-mile (800 meters) south of Ferndell, crammed with Thai restaurants, markets, stores, and massage spas. South of Hollywood Boulevard lies **Little Armenia**, home to a sizeable Armenian-American community since the 1970s; highlights include the St Garabed Armenian Apostolic Church on Alexandria Avenue.

Forest Lawn Hollywood Hills

hood home and now filled with trains of all scales, as well as Walt's personal items and tools. A little farther on, the **Travel Town Museum** ⑩ (5200 Zoo Drive; www.traveltown.org; Mon–Fri 10am–4pm, Sat & Sun 10am–6pm) maintains a lot full of creaky locomotives and antique trucks from all over Southern California.

FOREST LAWN HOLLYWOOD HILLS

Another mile (1.6km) on from Travel Town, adults might prefer to wander the landscaped grounds of **Forest Lawn Hollywood Hills** ⑪ (6300 Forest Lawn Drive; https://forestlawn.com; daily 8am–5pm; free). This cemetery of the stars offers poignant memorials to such figures as Gene Autry, Albert 'Cubby' Broccoli, Bette Davis, Marvin Gaye, Buster Keaton, Stan Laurel, Liberace, and Jack Webb.

Hollywood Hills homes

HOLLYWOOD HILLS AND MULHOLLAND DRIVE

The Hollywood Hills edge the northern rim of LA, home to the city's most opulent homes. Mulholland Drive runs along the central ridge, offering a series of fabulous viewpoints and a chance to end up at the city's greatest art museum, the Getty Center.

DISTANCE: 15.5 miles (25km)
TIME: A full day
START: Hollywood Bowl
END: Getty Center
POINTS TO NOTE: This route can only be traveled by car; once on Mulholland Drive, traffic should be relatively light, but try to avoid weekends, or Mondays, if you intend to visit the museums.

The Hollywood Hills are both a geographical feature, part of the Santa Monica Mountains that wrap around the northern side of LA, and also a hillside neighborhood north of Hollywood, where mansions are so commonplace that only the half-dozen full-blown castles really stand out. Constructed in 1924, 24-mile (39km) Mulholland Drive was the creation of Water Bureau Chief and City Engineer, William D. Mulholland, who envisaged a scenic road boosting the city's nascent tourist industry. Immortalized by the 2001 David Lynch movie *Mulholland Drive*, the winding route starts west of the 101

Freeway in Hollywood, and offers panoramic city, mountain, and ocean views all the way to I-405 in Bel Air.

HOLLYWOOD HILLS

Start out at the **Hollywood Bowl** ❶ (www.hollywoodbowl.com) at 2301 N Highland Avenue, just off US-101. This natural amphitheater in the Hollywood Hills is best known for its open-air auditorium; the Beatles played here in the mid-1960s, but the Bowl's principal function is as the occasional summer home of the Los Angeles Philharmonic (www.laphil.com).

An overview of the Bowl's history can be gleaned from the video inside the **Hollywood Bowl Museum** (late June–late Sept Tue–Sat 10am–showtime, Sun 4pm–showtime, late Sept–late June Tue–Fri 10am–5pm; free) near the entrance. With a collection of musical instruments from around the world, the museum also features recordings of notable symphonic moments in the Bowl's history and architectural drawings by Lloyd Wright, Frank's son, who contributed a design for one of its many bandshells. From here drive

Arriving at the Skirball Cultural Center

one mile (1.6km) north along Cahuenga Boulevard to the Cahuenga Pass and the turn off to Mulholland Drive.

MULHOLLAND DRIVE

Mulholland Drive runs west along the mountain crest from Cahuenga Pass, providing magnificent vistas of the Los Angeles basin and the San Fernando Valley; at night, both spread out like sparkling grids for miles below. Signposted viewpoints, usually with ample parking, line the route, beginning with the **Jerome C. Daniel Overlook above the Hollywood Bowl ❷**. As its name suggest, there's a beautiful view of the Hollywood Bowl itself, and, on a clear day, the ocean and Catalina Island. To the east,

the **Hollywood Sign** (see page 89) and Griffith Park Observatory should also be clearly visible. If you fancy stretching your legs, drive on to the **Runyon Canyon ❸** parking lot, where hiking trails make moderately steep loops along the ridge. Continue to the **Universal City Overlook ❹**, which provides a viewpoint north into the San Fernando Valley. Two miles (3.2km) on, the **Nancy Hoover Pohl Overlook at Fryman Canyon ❺** provides similar vistas, but is a better place to take a break, with access to the canyon trails below. The stop honors local activist Nancy Hoover Pohl, who was instrumental in creating scenic Fryman Canyon Park below.

The next stretch of Mulholland contains more scenic overlooks, the best

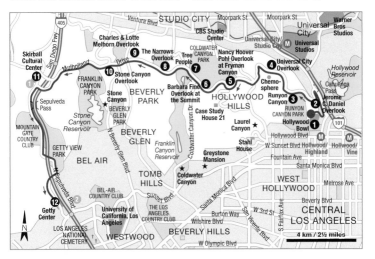

Living the high life, Stahl House

of which is the **Barbara Fine Overlook at the Summit** ❻, the beginning of a short trail to spots with stunning perspectives on the upper fork of Fryman Canyon, the San Fernando Valley, the Simi Hills, and the San Gabriel Mountains. Another 0.8 miles (1.3km) along Mulholland you'll pass the entrance to **Tree People** ❼ (www.treepeople. org; 6.30am–sunset; free), located in 45-acre (18-hectare) Coldwater Can-

yon Park. This environmental nonprofit organization runs a variety of tours and programs in the park aimed at encouraging conservation, and its grounds make for a tranquil hike.

Continue to **The Narrows Overlook** ❽, another viewpoint looking north over the San Fernando Valley, and another mile (1.6km) beyond that to the **Charles & Lotte Melhorn Overlook** ❾ over Deep Canyon. At the **Stone Canyon Overlook** ❿, the view is once again to the south, this time of beautiful Stone Canyon Reservoir in Bel Air and the ocean beyond.

Skirball Cultural Center

It's another 2.3 miles (3.7km) to the **Skirball Cultural Center** ⓫ (www.skirball.org; Mon–Fri noon–5pm, Sat & Sun 10am–5pm; free parking) at 2701 N Sepulveda Boulevard (just off Mulholland and across I-405). This Jewish cultural center contains museum galleries and offers a range of courses, readings, and talks. Israeli architect Moshe Safdie designed the handsome 15-acre (6-hectare) campus, a series of building clusters and a network of outdoor courtyards, arcades, and landscaped ravines within the hills. Winnick Hall contains the Getty Gallery, Family Art Studio, and Noah's Ark, a floor-to-ceiling wooden ark filled with whimsical animals, specially designed for kids to explore. The 'Visions and Values' exhibition displays work from the Skirball's permanent collection of Judaica – one of the largest

Architectural wonders

The architectural highlights of the Hollywood Hills include the **Chemosphere**, a giant UFO house hovering above the canyon on a long pedestal, designed by quirky architect John Lautner in 1960; and **Case Study House #21** (or Bailey House), Pierre Koenig's 1959 hillside glass-and-steel box, part of the influential Case Study Program that tried to bring Modernism to the middle class in the 1940s and 50s. Koenig's other notable home, **Case Study House #22** (also 1959), known as the Stahl House, has an even more spectacular layout, famously perched above a cliff. Best of all, the house is on view for occasional one-hour tours (www.stahlhouse.com). Unfortunately, most of the area's other houses are hidden away, and there's no real way to explore in depth without your own car, a copy of the latest *Thomas Guide* map and, if possible, a detailed LA architecture guide.

The sleek Getty Center   *The Hollywood Sign*

in the world. Take a break at the on-site **Zeidler's Café**, see ❶.

THE GETTY CENTER

It's definitely worth making time for the **Getty Center** ⓬ (www.getty.edu; Tue–Fri & Sun 10am–5.30pm, Sat 10am–9pm; free), 3.5 miles (5.6km) south of the Skirball Center via I-405. The monumental art center, a gleaming 110-acre (45-hectare) complex, towers over the city. Oil baron J. Paul Getty started building his massive collection in the 1930s, storing much of it in his house, now the Getty Villa (see page 48), until the Getty Center opened in 1974 on a bluff overlooking the Pacific Ocean. Designed by arch-Modernist Richard Meier, the Center was built in classical travertine for about $1 billion. The collection is massive; highlights include Correggio's *Head of Christ*, Titian's *Portrait of Alfonso d'Avalos*, several excellent Rembrandts, and *Irises* by Van Gogh. Pause at the Getty's restaurant or make for upscale **The Bel-Air**, see ❷, which lies just across I-405.

The Hollywood Sign

Originally, when it was built in 1923, the famed **Hollywood Sign** (https://hollywoodsign.org) read 'Hollywoodland' and was an advertisement for a real estate development. However, over the course of half a century, the sign, designed to stand for only 18 months, sustained extensive damage and deterioration; the 'land' part was removed and the rest became the familiar symbol it is today.

There's no vehicular access to the sign (Beachwood Drive comes nearest), though it is possible to hike along the access road that cuts behind the sign to the summit of Mount Lee. Don't try and get any closer; razor wire fence, infrared cameras, and radar-activated zoom lenses have been installed to catch graffiti writers, and innocent tourists who can't resist a closer peek are also liable for a steep fine.

Food and Drink

❶ ZEIDLER'S CAFÉ

2701 N Sepulveda Boulevard (Skirball Cultural Center); tel: 310-440 4515; Tue–Sat 11.30am–3.30pm; $$
The Skirball Center's spacious café serves kosher Californian cuisine, from gourmet sandwiches and salads to lox and eggs, pasta, and pizza.

❷ THE BEL-AIR

662 N Sepulveda Boulevard; tel: 310-440 5544; www.thebel-air.com; Mon–Fri 11.30am–3pm & 4–9pm, Sat 5–10pm; $$$
Upscale restaurant serving contemporary Californian fusion cusine such as potato latkes, turkey bolognese, and sesame-crusted ahi tuna, as well as their famous Bel-Air chopped salad.

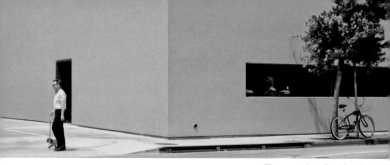

The eye-catching Paul Smith store

MELROSE, WEST HOLLYWOOD, AND THE SUNSET STRIP

A tour of the hip boutiques of Melrose, restaurants and design showcases of West Hollywood, and the rock legends of the Sunset Strip makes for one of LA's most enticing days out.

DISTANCE: 2.5 miles (4km)
TIME: A full day
START: Melrose Avenue
END: Sunset Strip
POINTS TO NOTE: This route is easily completed on foot, with most locations also accessible by bus (the DASH Fairfax service runs along much of Melrose Avenue; bus No. 2 runs along Sunset).

Melrose District became a popular underground and new wave shopping area in the early 1980s as the epicenter of Southern California's punk culture. Today 'The New Rodeo Drive' is more about upscale boutiques that indie stores. Neighboring **West Hollywood** is synonymous with design, social tolerance, and upscale trendiness, and has a sizeable LGBTQ contingent. Above West Hollywood, the conglomeration of restaurants, plush hotels, and nightclubs on Sunset Boulevard has long been known as the **Sunset Strip**. The Strip came to national fame in the 1960s when a scene developed around the landmark **Whisky-a-Go-Go** club, which hosted seminal rock bands such as Love, Buffalo Springfield, and The Doors.

MELROSE AVENUE

Melrose Avenue is LA's trendiest shopping street, in its heyday an eccentric world of underground art galleries, palm readers, and head shops. Since the 1990s, a crush of designer boutiques and restaurants has been gaining ground, though there are still enough eye-popping stores to make for an interesting stroll.

The main shopping district runs for almost 2 miles (3.2km), from North La Brea Avenue to La Cienega Boulevard; purists will want to walk the whole district, but for an abridged tour, begin at **Melrose Trading Post ❶** outdoor flea market (www.melrosetradingpost.org; Sun 9am–5pm). If it's not a Sunday, head to Melrose and Edinburgh, where landmark vintage fashion stores **Reformation** (8000 Melrose Avenue) and **Chuck's Vintage ❷** (No. 8012) carry the city's best selection of jeans, t-shirts, Victorian dresses, and army wear. Walk

Whisky a Go Go has launched bands from The Doors to Guns N' Roses

west two blocks to the legendary **Fred Segal** ❸ flagship (www.fredsegal.com; Mon–Sat 10am–9pm, Sun 11am–6pm) at No. 8500, a one-stop lifestyle store that has been at the heart of LA pop culture since 1961. On-site **Fred Segal Mauro's Café**, see ❶, is a favorite with Hollywood's movers and shakers. Continue to the multi-colored boutique of **Paul Smith** ❹ (No. 8221; Mon–Sat 11am–7pm, Sun noon–6pm). **Vivienne Westwood** ❺ holds court at No. 8320, with **Rebecca Minkoff's** mural-adorned handbag emporium across the street at No. 8335.

Take a retail break by walking a couple of blocks north up Kings Road to the **MAK Center for Art and Architecture** ❻ (www.makcenter.org; Wed–Sun 11am–6pm) at No. 835, which hosts a range of avant-garde music, art, film, and design exhibitions. The center occupies the 1922 Schindler House, for years the blueprint of California Modernist architecture. Back on Melrose, the Kardashian sisters' boutique **DASH** ❼ (Mon–Sat 11am–7pm, Sun noon–6pm) stands at No. 8420, selling high-end women's designer brands.

Melrose Place

Melrose Place branches off Melrose Avenue just before DASH (Melrose Place Farmers Market sets up at this junction every Sunday), lined with two blocks of posh boutiques. Highlights include beloved **Alfred Coffee**; **The Row** ❽

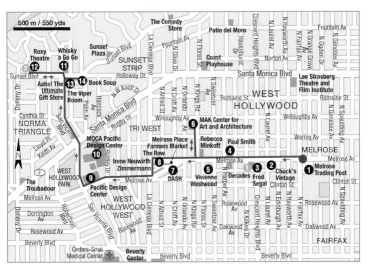

Pacific Design Center

(No. 8440), Ashley and Mary-Kate Olsen's fashion boutique; women's clothes at **Zimmermann** (No. 8468); and the ocean-inspired jewelry designs of SoCal native **Irene Neuwirth** (No. 8458).

WEST HOLLYWOOD

At the end of Melrose Place, turn left (south) on La Cienaga to return to Melrose Avenue, continuing west into the **West Hollywood Design District**, known for its galleries, furniture designers, and yet more fashion boutiques. The west end of Melrose is dominated by the hulking, bright-blue glassy pile of the **Pacific Design Center** ❾ (No. 8687; www.pacificdesigncenter.com; Mon–Fri 9am–5pm), a marketplace for over 100 art galleries and stores. It sits alongside its counterparts, the geometric Green Building (1988) and Red Building (2012) superblocks. Don't miss the much more understated **MOCA Pacific Design Center** ❿ (www.moca.org; Tue–Fri 11am–5pm, Sat & Sun 11am–6pm; free), which focuses on architecture and design with a sleek, modern bent.

SUNSET STRIP

From the design center, it's a 15-minute walk north along San Vicente Boulevard to Sunset Boulevard, better known here as the **Sunset Strip**. On the corner is **Aahs! The Ultimate Gift Store** (8878 Sunset Boulevard), while opposite is the legendary **Whisky a Go Go** ⓫ at No. 8901. The club opened in 1964, sparking the careers of numerous bands over the years, from The Byrds and The Doors to the Red Hot Chili Peppers. It remains at the heart of what's left of the strip's rock scene. A couple of blocks west you can grab a drink or dinner at the grungy **Rainbow Bar and Grill**, see ❷, while the neighboring **Roxy Theatre** ⓬ (No. 9009; www.theroxy.com) opened in 1973, staging the US premier of the *Rocky Horror Show* one year later.

To the east, Johnny Depp was one of the original founders of **The Viper Room** ⓭ (www.viperroom.com) at No. 8852; in its heyday it hosted the likes of Johnny Cash, Bruce Springsteen, and Sheryl Crow. Non-rockers should continue on to No. 8818, where **Book Soup** ⓮ (www.book soup.com) is an excellent bookstore, and the clutch of restaurants beyond.

Food and Drink

❶ FRED SEGAL MAURO'S CAFÉ

8112 Melrose Avenue; tel: 323-653 7970; www.mauroscafe.com; Mon–Sat 9am–6pm, Sun 9am–5pm; $$

Known for its exquisite Italian food but also for its celebrity clientele.

❷ RAINBOW BAR AND GRILL

9015 Sunset Boulevard; tel: 310-278 4232; www.rainbowbarandgrill.com; Daily 11am–2am; $$

Celeb hangout offering reasonably priced burgers, pizzas, and Mexican food.

The iconic Sunset Strip

UCLA

WESTWOOD AND UCLA

Westwood, along with the UCLA campus in West LA, is the city's fun student center, with cheap restaurants and bars enhanced by some high-quality art museums, gardens, and beautiful Spanish Revival architecture.

DISTANCE: 2 miles (3.2km)
TIME: A full day
START: Westwood Village Memorial Park
END: Murphy Sculpture Garden
POINTS TO NOTE: If you're planning to visit any of the museums, avoid doing this walk on a Monday or Tuesday. Metro bus lines 2/302, 20, 720, 734 and 788 serve UCLA and Westwood. If you drive here, note that street parking is limited and expensive; for minimum frustration, find a cheap parking lot and dump your vehicle there while you explore. The route itself can be easily completed on foot.

Just west of Beverly Hills, Westwood is one of LA's more walkable neighborhoods, a grouping of low-slung Spanish Revival buildings that went up in the late 1920s. It's based around Broxton Avenue, along with the nearby campus of University of California, Los Angeles (UCLA), established here in 1929. Initially a relatively low-key neighborhood, in the 1960s and 1970s Westwood rose to become LA's nightlife and entertainment hub, a

rare pedestrian-friendly zone in a city built for cars. Following a period of decline, Westwood has been reviving since the early 2000s. On the northern side of Westwood, the 419-acre (170-hectare) UCLA campus comprises a group of lovely Romanesque Revival structures and modern buildings spread across well-landscaped grounds; this route covers the highlights, but there's a lot more to see – start at www.ucla.edu/visit.

WESTWOOD

Start on Wilshire Boulevard, where it meets Westwood Boulevard, the neighborhood's main drag. Just to the south on Glendon Avenue, **Westwood Village Memorial Park ❶** (www.dignitymemorial.com; daily 8am–5pm) is tucked away between the office buildings, the resting place of some of Hollywood's biggest stars. Formally established in 1905, this area had been used for burials since the 1880s. Today it contains memorials to movie stars Jack Lemon, Farrah Fawcett, Natalie Wood, Burt Lancaster, and Dean Martin, authors Truman Capote and Ray

Bradbury, jazz drummer Buddy Rich, and, to the left of the entrance in the far northeast corner, Marilyn Monroe, who rests under a lipstick-covered plaque (*Playboy* founder Hugh Hefner paid $75,000 for the crypt next to her).

Return to Wilshire and cross the street to UCLA's **Hammer Museum** ❷ (https://hammer.ucla.edu; 10899 Wilshire Boulevard; Tue–Fri 11am–8pm, Sat & Sun 11am–5pm; free). The museum owns the largest collection of works by French satirist Honoré Daumier outside of Paris, as well as a cache of minor works by Titian, Rembrandt, and Rubens. Founded in 1990 by businessman Armand Hammer, it also contains his personal collection of 19th-century French art, including works by Degas, Cézanne, Gauguin, Van Gogh, and Pissarro.

From here, walk north along Westwood Boulevard, taking in the scene. The 1929

Bel Air

One of the most famous, affluent communities in America, **Bel Air** blankets the hillsides north of Westwood, boasting one of the most exquisite hotels in the LA region, *Hotel Bel Air* (owned by the Sultan of Brunei), and the most exclusive club, the Bel-Air Country Club. Incidentally, though Will Smith's breakthrough TV sitcom *The Fresh Prince of Bel Air* was set here in the early 1990s, the exterior shots were filmed in nearby Brentwood (and the show was filmed entirely in studios).

Janss Dome ❸ lies just beyond Kinross Avenue, its Moorish dome a neighborhood icon. Continue walking north along Broxton Avenue, which forks off Westwood Avenue here, up to the historic **Fox Village Theater** ❹ at No. 961. Opened in 1931, the Spanish Mission-style movie theater features an iconic 170ft (52-meter) spire topped with an Art Deco 'Fox' sign. Today it's still operating under the Regency Theatres umbrella. Grab a coffee or delicious sweet snack at Stan's Corner Donut Shoppe (10948 Weyburn Avenue, at Broxton; www.stansdoughnuts.com), or lunch at **BJ's Restaurant & Brewhouse**, see ❶.

Continue north and turn right on Le Conte Avenue to reach another historic theater at No. 10886. **The Geffen Playhouse** ❺ (www.geffenplayhouse.org) was completed in 1929 as a UCLA students and alumni club, and was converted into a theater in the 1990s. On the other side of Le Conte lies the sprawling UCLA campus.

UCLA

Start your tour of the UCLA campus by walking east along Le Conte Avenue to Hilgard Avenue and the entrance to **Mildred E. Mathias Botanical Garden** ❻ (www.botgard.ucla.edu/self-guided-tours; Mon–Fri 8am–5pm, Sat & Sun 8am–4pm; free). This bucolic glade contains almost 4,000 rare and native species; pick your way along sloping paths through the redwoods and fern groves, past small waterfalls

Students at the Powell Library

splashing into lily-covered ponds.

Exit the Garden at the northern end on Charles E. Young Drive and look for the steps and alley to the left of the Biomedical Sciences Research Building. Continue walking north through the Court of Sciences to the Geology Building on the right, home to one of the quirkier sights on campus. Located in room 3697, the **Meteorite Gallery ⑦** (Mon–Fri 9am–4pm, Sun 1–4pm) exhibits about 100 actual meteorite samples from the university's collection of over 1,500. Continuing north you should emerge on Portola Plaza, with the majestic **Powell Library ⑧** ahead, a 1929 Romanesque Revival beauty. Before going in take a break at the **Kerckhoff Coffee House**, see ②, inside the UCLA Bruincard Center on the left. Inside the library, the spellbinding interior features graceful arches, columns, and stairwells, and an array of medieval ornaments to complement its ecclesiastical feel. The highlight is the dome above the read-

ing room, where Renaissance printers' marks are inscribed, among them icons

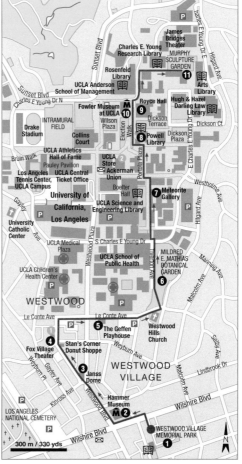

The UCLA Bruins in action

representing such pioneers as Johann Fust and William Caxton. Immediately to the north is the monumental **Royce Hall** ❾ (www.roycehall.org), another original from 1929 and its twin-towered facade a university landmark. Today it is the main concert venue on campus.

The Fowler Museum at UCLA

The building to the west of Royce Hall is the **Fowler Museum at UCLA** ❿ (www.fowler.ucla.edu; Wed noon–8pm, Thu–Sun noon–5pm; free), which displays objects representing the ancient, traditional, and contemporary cultures of Africa, Native and Latin America, Asia, and the Pacific Ocean – everything from the complex batik textiles of Indonesia and the vivid papier-mâché sculptures of Mexico, to Yoruba beaded arts of Nigeria, and pre-Columbian ceramic vessels of Peru. From here it's a short walk through the campus to the **Murphy Sculpture Garden** ⓫, containing 70 works by such major names as Jean Arp, Henry Moore, Henri Matisse, and Jacques Lipchitz. Highlights include *Two-Piece Reclining Figure, No. 3* (1961) by Henry Moore, *Baigneuse* (Bather; 1923–25) by Jacques Lipchitz, and *Walking Man* (1877–78) by Rodin, his famous nude composed of only a torso and legs. Look out also for *Amazonian Standing Woman* by Gaston Lachaise, a proud, voluptuous 1933 bronze sculpture. From here the nearest bus stops are on Hilgard Avenue.

Food and Drink

❶ BJ'S RESTAURANT & BREWHOUSE

939 Broxton Avenue; tel: 310-209 7475; www.bjsrestaurants.com; Mon–Thu 11am–midnight, Fri 11am–12.30am, Sat 10am–12.30am, Sun 10am–midnight; $$

The best of the mostly chain restaurants in central Westwood, this is a favorite of UCLA students for its well-priced burgers, pizzas, salads, and steaks, plus a decent range of beers.

❷ KERCKHOFF COFFEE HOUSE

Kerckhoff Hall, 2nd Floor (UCLA campus); tel: 310-206 0729; Mon–Thu 7am–11pm, Fri 7am–7pm, Sat 8am–6pm, Sun 8am–11pm; $

UCLA's first coffee house, opened in 1976, remains a campus institution. Best for espresso coffee drinks, but also serves pastries, homemade soups, gourmet salads, and sandwiches.

The UCLA Bruins and the Hall of Fame

UCLA's sports teams are known as the **Bruins** (www.uclabruins.com), their biggest rivals the USC Trojans (see page 81). You can learn more about the sporting traditions of UCLA at the **Athletics Hall of Fame** (Mon–Fri 8am–5pm) on campus in the J. D. Morgan Center (just east of Pauley Pavilion and west of the UCLA Store at Ackerman Union).

Touring the UCLA campus

LONG BEACH AND SAN PEDRO

Marine life and maritime history are celebrated at the port cities of Long Beach and San Pedro, home to top-notch aquariums, whale-watching trips, and famous vessels such as the Queen Mary and the battleship SS Iowa.

DISTANCE: 5.5 miles (8km) in Long Beach; 6.5 miles (10.5km) to San Pedro; 4.5 miles (7.2km) in San Pedro
TIME: Two days
START: Long Beach Museum of Art
END: Cabrillo Marine Aquarium
POINTS TO NOTE: With so many attractions in Long Beach and San Pedro, at least two days are recommended for this route – a stay in Long Beach for a night or two will save the journey from other parts of LA. The route can be completed with a combination of walking and public transportation, or by car. The Metro Blue Line runs between the Downtown Long Beach station and the 7th Street/Metro Center station in Downtown LA. The free 'Passport' shuttle bus runs to the Aquarium of the Pacific, Pine Avenue, Shoreline Village, and the *Queen Mary*.

One of the largest ports in the world, Long Beach is also the region's second-largest city, with nearly half a million people. Once mostly ranchland, the town emerged as a beach resort in the early 20th century before becoming increasingly associated with the oil industry. Today, Downtown Long Beach, 25 miles (40km) south of Downtown LA, is quite flashy, with office buildings, a conference center, hotels, a shopping mall, and some of the best-preserved early 20th-century buildings on the coast.

Linked to Long Beach by the 1,500ft (457-meter) Vincent Thomas Bridge across the harbor, the port of San Pedro was a small fishing community until the late 19th century, when the construction of the Port of Los Angeles nearby brought a huge influx of foreign labor. Many of these immigrants, and their descendants, never left the place, lending a discernable multicultural mix to the town.

LONG BEACH

Start with a morning on the **beach**, taking in the vistas and sea breezes below the **Long Beach Museum of Art ❶** (2300 E Ocean Boulevard; www.lbma.org; Thu 11am–8pm, Fri–Sun 11am–5pm). On the weekend you can

Robert Wyland's life-sized whales adorn the Long Beach Convention Center

grab breakfast on the lovely terrace (with ocean views) at **Claire's At the Museum**, see ❶. Set in a magnificent clifftop home built in 1912, the museum itself displays changing exhibitions in a variety of mediums, some from its eclec-

tic permanent collection of everything from English Staffordshire figurative ceramics to California Modernism and contemporary art of California.

From here it's a stiff 1.6-mile (2.6km) walk inland to the next attraction, best cov-

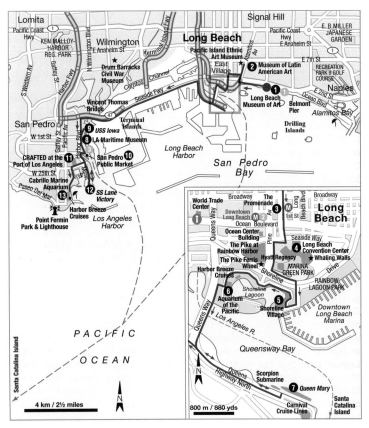

Colorful fish at the Aquarium of the Pacific

ered by taxi or by car; if art isn't your thing, take a No. 121 bus along Ocean Boulevard straight to The Promenade in Downtown Long Beach (see below). Art lovers should proceed to the **Museum of Latin American Art ❷** (628 Alamitos Avenue; www.molaa.org; Wed–Sun 11am–5pm, Fri until 9pm), LA's only major museum devoted solely to Latino art, including big names like Mexican muralist José Orozco. Opposite, at No. 695, the **Pacific Island Ethnic Art Museum** (www.pieam.org; Wed–Sun 11am–5pm) focuses on the art of the Pacific islands but especially the culture of Micronesia. To get to the Promenade from here, take bus No. 91 from East 6th Street and Olive, or walk south on Alamitos Avenue, then west on East 3rd Street, through the heart of the **East Village Arts District** (a neighborhood of indie shops and galleries).

DOWNTOWN LONG BEACH

Beginning at 3rd Street, the three-block strip known as **The Promenade ❸** runs south to Ocean Boulevard, lined with touristy restaurants and stores that can get busy on weekend nights. **Pier 76 Fish Grill**, see ❷, is a great place for lunch. Keeping walking south on Pine Avenue, with **Long Beach Convention Center ❹** on your left, and turn left into **Rainbow Lagoon Park** (you can also take the 'Passport' shuttle bus). Once you reach the lagoon itself you should get a view of one of the world's largest murals, surrounding the circular main auditorium of the convention center. This behemoth (dubbed 'Planet Ocean') was completed in 1992 and belongs to artist Robert Wyland's famed **Whaling Walls** series, all featuring life-size whales. Cross Shoreline Drive to head into **Shoreline Village ❺** (https://shorelinevillage.com; daily 10am–9pm), a waterfront entertainment complex featuring shops, funfair arcades, and restaurants. It's a short walk along the harbor east from here to the Aquarium of the Pacific.

Aquarium of the Pacific

The most popular family attraction in Long Beach is the **Aquarium of the Pacific ❻** (100 Aquarium Way; www.aquariumofpacific.org; daily 9am–6pm), which exhibits more than 11,000 marine species from the Pacific region, from the familiar sea lions and otters, tide-pool creatures, and assorted ocean flora, to the more exotic leopard sharks and giant Japanese spider crabs. The aquarium's interactive Shark Lagoon is especially fun (kids can touch the gentle bamboo and epaulette

---

San Pedro Trolley

A trio of classic 1908 Pacific Electric Red Cars (two replica trolley buses, one restored), the free **San Pedro Downtown Trolley** links most of the city's major attractions (www.sptrolley.com; early May–early Sept Sat noon–6pm, Sun noon–8pm). Check the website for the current schedule.

A busy day on Santa Catalina Island

sharks), while visitors can also feed the tropical Australian parrots in Lorikeet Forest. From the aquarium, take the 'Passport' shuttle bus to the *Queen Mary* (1.2 miles/1.9km away).

THE QUEEN MARY

Long Beach's most famous attraction is, of course, the mighty *Queen Mary* ❼ (1126 Queens Highway; www.queenmary.com; Mon–Thu 10am–6pm, Fri–Sun 10am–7pm), the 1936 Art Deco ocean liner purchased by the city of Long Beach in 1967. Now a luxury hotel, the ship is also open for exhibits that include extravagantly furnished lounges and luxurious first-class cabins, and a wealth of gorgeous Art Deco details in its glasswork, geometric décor, and chic streamlining; there are also shops and restaurants and even a wedding chapel. Make sure you visit the **Observation Bar**.

> ## Long Beach whale-watching trips
>
> Between November and March, more than 15,000 grey and fin whales (and large numbers of blue whales) cruise the 'Whale Freeway' past Long Beach on their annual migration to and from winter breeding and birthing grounds in Baja California. **Harbor Breeze Cruises** (www.longbeachcruises.com) operates good two-hour whale- and dolphin-watching trips.

SAN PEDRO

Commuter bus No. 142 links Long Beach at Ocean Boulevard with Downtown San Pedro (20 minutes) and the **LA Maritime Museum** ❽ (Berth 84, at the western edge of 6th Street; www.lamaritimemuseum.org; Tue–Sun 10am–5pm), the best place to start your tour. Inside are art and artifacts from the glory days of San Pedro's fishing and whaling industries, with displays on everything from old-fashioned clipper-ship voyages to contemporary diving expeditions. Just to the north, along the harborfront, the giant battleship **USS Iowa** ❾ (250 S Harbor Boulevard; https://pacificbattleship.com; daily 10am–5pm) served throughout World War II and the Korean War, finally being decommissioned in 1990. In 2012 she was berthed here and has been comprehensively restored, with the interior loaded with exhibits about life and war at sea.

Retrace your steps and walk south (or take the San Pedro Trolley) along the waterfront to the former site of Ports O'Call Village; in 2018 this tourist mall was torn down to be replaced by a flashy new development dubbed **San Pedro Public Market** ❿, slated for completion in 2020. Restaurant **San Pedro Fish Market**, see ❸, will be open throughout. If it's a Friday or a weekend, take the San Pedro Trolley on to **CRAFTED at the Port of Los Angeles** ⓫ (www.craftedportla.com; Fri–Sun 11am–6pm), an arts and crafts market. Continue for just under a mile south to

Into the deep

the **SS *Lane Victory*** ⓬ at berth 49 (3600 Miner Street; https://thelanevictory.org; Fri–Wed 9am–4pm), a huge, 10,000-ton cargo ship that was built in the shipyard in 1945 and operated in Korea and Vietnam. Tours take you through its many cramped spaces, including the engine and radio rooms, crew quarters, galley, and bridge.

With more time you can continue farther south around the harbor to the **Cabrillo Marine Aquarium** ⓭ (3720 Stephen White Drive; www.cabrillomarine aquarium.org; Tue–Fri noon–5pm, Sat & Sun 10am–5pm), displaying a diverse collection of marine life: everything from predator snails, octopuses, and jellyfish to larger displays on otters, seals, and whales. Frank Gehry designed the main building in 1981.

Santa Catalina Island

The enticing island of **Santa Catalina**, 22 miles (35km) long and 20 miles (32km) offshore from Long Beach, is mostly preserved wilderness grazed by a herd of 150 bison (said to be descendants of animals brought over for a movie shoot in 1924). The island has substantial charm, and provides a stark contrast to the metropolis, with unspoiled cycling, hiking, and scuba diving on offer. Indeed, with cars largely forbidden, the 4,000 islanders walk, ride bicycles, or drive golf carts. Fast ferries run from Long Beach Downtown Landing (1hr) and San Pedro (1hr 15min) to Avalon (the main town) with Catalina Express at least four times daily (www.catalinaexpress.com). The Visitor Center (www.catalinachamber. com; daily 9am–5pm) is located at the foot of the Green Pier in Avalon.

Food and Drink

① CLAIRE'S AT THE MUSEUM

2300 E Ocean Boulevard, Long Beach; tel: 562-439 2119; www.lbma.org/claires; Thu 11am–8pm, Fri 11am–3pm, Sat & Sun 8am–3pm; $$
The ocean views from the outdoor terrace make this café at the Long Beach Museum of Art the perfect place for breakfast or lunch (think fluffy omelettes, steak and eggs, breakfast burritos, etc).

② PIER 76 FISH GRILL

95 Pine Avenue, Long Beach; tel: 562-983 1776; www.pier76fishgrill.com; Sun–Thu 11am–9pm, Sat & Sun 11am–9.30pm; $$
Local seafood institution just off The Promenade, with a huge range of grilled fresh fish, steamed mussels, chowder, smoked fish tacos, and lobster rolls.

③ SAN PEDRO FISH MARKET

1190 Nagoya Way, San Pedro; tel: 310-832 4251; www.sanpedrofish.com; daily 8am–8pm; $$
Seafood restaurant right on the waterfront (with a massive outdoor terrace), locally renowned since 1955 for its fried shrimp tray and fresh fish counter.

DIRECTORY

Hand-picked hotels and restaurants to suit all budgets and tastes, organised by area, plus select nightlife listings, an alphabetical listing of practical information, and an overview of the best books and films to give you a flavor of the city.

Room at the Figueroa Hotel

ACCOMMODATIONS

Los Angeles has plenty of accommodations, from budget motels to world-class resorts. The city is so big that the area in which you stay will have a big impact on your travel plans. Downtown, the historic heart of the city, has both chic hotels and basic dives, but getting to the coast from here can be a hassle; Hollywood and West Hollywood are safe, relatively central options for seeing the whole city, while Santa Monica and Venice are predominantly mid-to-upper-range territory, perfect for soaking up the beach culture but a long way from the cultural attractions inland.

Prices fluctuate considerably in Los Angeles; they are most commonly dictated by demand and location, and less so by season, as the city tends to be busy year-round. Be that as it may, March to May and September to November do tend to be less crowded, with the best weather and mild temperatures. Between the Christmas and Easter/Spring break periods (January and February) you might find some bargains, though the weather tends to be cool (and even rainy) at this time. Some inland hotels also offer discounts in July and August when temperatures soar, though hotels in the oceanside neighborhoods are at a premium at this time of year.

Downtown LA

Figueroa Hotel
939 S Figueroa Street; tel: 213-627 8971; www.hotelfigueroa.com;
$$$
This onetime YWCA (built in 1925, financed, owned, and later operated by women) has been transformed into a stylish hotel with hardwood flooring and arty metal detail. There's a pool out back for enjoying the Californian sun.

Hilton Checkers
535 S Grand Avenue; tel: 213-624 0000; www.hilton.com; $$$
Historic and intimate deluxe boutique hotel, designed in a whimsical Spanish Mission Revival style by Charles Whittlesey and opened in 1927 as the 'Mayflower.' Rooms are elegantly appointed with antiques and fine artwork. Contains gourmet restaurant Checker's Downtown and lobby bar, rooftop pool, and Jacuzzi.

> Price for a standard double room for one night without breakfast in high season:
> $ = below $100
> $$ = $100–200
> $$$ = $200–300
> $$$$ = above $300

The Westin Bonaventure Hotel & Suites

The Inn at 657

657 & 663 W 23rd Street; tel: 213-741 2200; https://theinnat657la.com; $$

Excellent B&B, halfway between Downtown and Exposition Park (just off I-110), with five smart, modern suites in the main, elegant 1900 building, and six in the newer one, which has a/c and en-suite bathrooms.

Luxe City Center Hotel

1020 S Figueroa Street; tel: 213-748 1291; https://luxecitycenter.com; $$$

Chic, Downtown chain hotel that offers sleek, contemporary decor, soothing tones and a host of amenities, including free use of local Gold's gym. The patio lounge, Nixo, features live bands and cocktails.

The Metric Hotel

285 Lucas Avenue; tel: 213-481 8181; www.metrichotel.com; $$

Formerly Jerry's Motel, the Metric will open as a new budget boutique hotel in mid-2019, with stylish rooms, free parking and free Wi-Fi. Family-run and just outside Downtown, this is a bargain.

Omni Los Angeles Hotel

251 S Olive Street; tel: 213-617 3300; www.omnihotels.com; $$$

Sited next to MOCA, Downtown's cheeriest business hotel is brightened with artworks and contemporary design. Contains the Noé Bar, with its signature martinis and Downtown views, the lauded Noé Restaurant, health club, pool, and saunas.

Westin Bonaventure Hotel & Suites

404 S Figueroa Street; tel: 213-624 1000; www.thebonaventure.com; $$$

Postmodernist luxury hotel with five glass towers that resemble cocktail shakers, a six-story atrium crammed with shops and a 'lake,' and elegant rooms with floor-to-ceiling views. The 367ft (112-meter) Downtown landmark was completed in 1976 (and starred in the movie *True Lies* in 1993). A breathtaking exterior elevator ascends to the BonaVista rotating cocktail lounge. Also features an outdoor pool, executive floor, spa, and health club.

Hollywood

Hollywood Bed & Breakfast

1701 N Orange Grove Avenue; tel: 323-874 8017; www.hollywoodbandb.com; $$

Fun, convenient place to stay, this quirky B&B in a 1912 home looks a little like something out of *Dr Seuss*. It's close to all the action, with four cozy rooms and a small pool.

Hollywood Celebrity Hotel

1775 Orchid Avenue; tel: 323-850 6464; www.hotelcelebrity.com; $$

A good choice on the affordable boutique scene, with a great location in

central Hollywood and rooms with charming furnishings, Art Deco flourishes, plus free breakfast and Wi-Fi. The theme is maintained by vintage black-and-white photographs of movie stars and film posters from Hollywood's golden age.

Hollywood Orchid Suites
1753 Orchid Avenue; tel: 800-537 3052; www.orchidsuites.com; $$
Roomy suites very close to the most popular parts of Hollywood and adjacent to the massive Hollywood & Highland mall. Small outdoor (heated) pool and free parking included.

Hollywood Roosevelt Hotel
7000 Hollywood Boulevard; tel: 323-856 1970; www.thehollywoodroosevelt.com; $$$
Opened in 1927 and site of the first Academy Awards ceremony two years later, this historic hotel features classic Spanish-revival decor and movie-star memorabilia (Marilyn Monroe lived at the hotel for two years early in her career). The latest iteration of its luxurious rooms were designed by Yabu Pushelberg. The hotel contains lauded restaurant Public Kitchen & Bar; cocktail lounge and vintage bowling alley the Spare Room (daily 8pm–2am); and the 1960s-style Tropicana Pool & Café, with the famous mural at the bottom of the pool (the 'dancing commas') painted by David Hockney in 1987.

Magic Castle Hotel
7025 Franklin Avenue; tel: 323-851 0800; www.magiccastlehotel.com; $$$
Justly popular hotel boasting single rooms (with queen beds) and spacious one and two-bedroom suites in a neat, modern style – with heated pool, free breakfast, and snacks 24 hours a day (free ice cream from 2.30pm). Also provides access to the otherwise hard-to-get-into private Magic Castle Club.

Orange Drive Hostel
1764 N Orange Drive; tel: 323-850 0350; www.orangedrivehostel.com; $
Centrally located hostel (right behind the Chinese Theatre), offering tours to film studios, theme parks, and homes of the stars. Free Wi-Fi and breakfast, with singles, doubles, and single-sex dorms available.

Venice, Santa Monica, and Malibu

Ambrose
1255 20th Street, Santa Monica; tel: 310-315 1555; www.ambrosehotel.com; $$$$
Best upscale choice for inland Santa Monica, with Arts and Crafts-styled decor and boutique rooms that have free Wi-Fi; includes continental breakfast. Free car service (within 3 miles/4.8km of the hotel).

Cal Mar
220 California Street, Santa Monica; tel: 310-395 5555; www.calmarhotel.com; $$$

Good for its central location (a 10-minute walk from Santa Monica State Beach Park), and its spacious suites have dining rooms, kitchens, and balconies. There's a heated outdoor pool, fitness room, and airport shuttle too.

Channel Road Inn

219 W Channel Road, Pacific Palisades; tel: 310-459 1920; www.channelroadinn.com; $$$

B&B rooms in a romantic getaway nestled in lower Santa Monica Canyon (northwest of central Santa Monica), with ocean views, a hot tub, and free bicycle rental. Enjoy complimentary grapes and champagne in the sumptuous rooms, each priced according to its view. The hotel was built in 1910 by architect Frank T. Kegley, a rare West Coast example of a shingle-clad Colonial Revival home. It was moved to its current location in 1977; after a period of abandonment, the house was restored and opened as a bed and breakfast in 1989.

HI–Santa Monica

1436 2nd Street, Santa Monica; tel: 310-393 9913; www.hilosangeles.org; $

A few blocks from the beach and pier, this building was LA's Town Hall from 1887 to 1889, and retains its historic charm, with a pleasant inner courtyard, guest kitchen, and library – and 260 beds (private rooms and single-sex dorms). Reservations essential in summer.

Hotel Shangri-La

1301 Ocean Avenue, Santa Monica; tel: 310-394 2791; www.shangrila-hotel.com; $$$$

Stylish Art Deco design makes this 1939 beachside hotel near the Santa Monica Pier an architectural gem (it's a family-owned hotel and not related to the international Shangri-La chain). The hotel enjoys amenities including high-speed internet and sound systems, lavish suites with views of the ocean, elevated pool and cabanas, chic rooftop bar Onyx and gourmet restaurant The Dining Room.

Loews Santa Monica Beach Hotel

1700 Ocean Avenue, Santa Monica; tel: 310-458 6700; www.loewshotels.com/santa-monica; $$$$

Luxurious beachfront hotel with a five-story glass atrium and outdoor swimming pool, perched above the beach two blocks from Santa Monica Pier. The best rooms have ocean views with sleek, glass balconies. Includes fresh fish specialist Ocean & Vine, craft cocktails and views at Papillion lounge, sundeck, fitness room with steam and dry saunas, and bicycle and skate rentals.

Shutters on the Beach

1 Pico Boulevard, Santa Monica; tel: 310-458 0030; www.shuttersonthebeach.com; $$$$

The only hotel in Santa Monica right on the beach. Exquisitely appointed rooms

in luxury New England cottage-style setting. Public areas have fireplaces and original artwork. Excellent restaurants (1 Pico and Coast Beach Café), pool, Jacuzzi, sauna, health club, spa, and bicycle and skate rentals.

Venice Breeze Suites
2 Breeze Avenue, Venice; tel: 310-566 2222; www.venicebreezesuites.com; $$$
Excellent location right on the boardwalk with sensational roof deck and loft-like serviced apartments equipped with full kitchens (some with ocean views) and free Wi-Fi.

Beverly Hills

Beverly Hills Hotel
9641 Sunset Boulevard; tel: 310-276 2251; www.dorchestercollection.com; $$$$
The classic Hollywood five-star resort, the 'Pink Palace' was built in 1912, with a bold color scheme and Mediterranean Revival-style design, and surrounded by its own exotic gardens. Since 1996 it has been run as part of the Dorchester Collection. Rooms feature marbled bathrooms, private balconies, Jacuzzis, and other such luxuries, while the celebrated 'bungalows' are set out across the gardens. Dine at the famed Polo Lounge restaurant, its outdoor patio enhanced with palm trees and blossoms.

The Beverly Hilton
9876 Wilshire Boulevard; tel: 310-274 7777; www.beverlyhilton.com; $$$$

This prominent, geometric white hotel at the corner of Wilshire and Santa Monica boulevards was opened by Conrad Hilton himself in 1955. Rooms come with plasma TVs, boutique decoration, and balconies. Whitney Houston died here in 2012; on a lighter note it is the scene of the annual Golden Globes awards in January, and it boasts the largest heated pool in Beverly Hills.

Beverly Wilshire
9500 Wilshire Boulevard; tel: 310-275 5200; www.fourseasons.com/beverlywilshire; $$$$
Completed in 1928 in Italian Renaissance style, the elegant lobby of this historic hotel at the base of Rodeo Drive gives way to sumptuous rooms with plush furnishings and luxurious marble baths. Currently part of the Four Seasons stable, the hotel boasts an Olympic-sized swimming pool, posh spa with steam room and sauna, restaurant CUT by Wolfgang Puck (and adjacent CUT Lounge), and the Pool Bar & Café. The hotel was the primary setting for the movie *Pretty Woman* in 1990.

Four Seasons Los Angeles
300 South Doheny Drive; tel: 310-273 2222; www.fourseasons.com/losangeles; $$$$
Refined luxury accommodations with excellent service and lots of celebrity-watching potential. Rooms are well

The grand Beverly Wilshire

appointed and have small balconies and beautiful bathrooms. Excellent fourth-floor pool and outdoor gym, a spa, multilingual concierge, house car, iPads in every room, restaurants, and lively cocktail lounges.

Maison 140

140 S Lasky Drive; tel: 310-281 4000; www.maison140.com; $$$

Kelly Wearstler-designed hotel for hipsters, boasting rooms with contemporary French design, free Wi-Fi, plus salon, bar, fitness room, and complimentary breakfast. The property was formerly the home of Hollywood actresses Lillian and Dorothy Gish in the 1930s, who later converted the mansion into a boarding house for young actresses. Candlelit Bar Noir features a mix of red Fresh slipper chairs, Asian antiques, and Lucite stools.

Viceroy L'Ermitage Beverly Hills

9291 Burton Way; tel: 310-278 3344; www. viceroyhotelsandresorts.com/en/beverlyhills; $$$$

This highly acclaimed ultra-luxury hotel is modern-minimalist and high-tech. The stylish French bistro, Avec Nous, rooftop pool, spa, gym, and sauna are second only to the accommodations, which start at 650 sq ft (60 sq meters) and come with huge bathrooms, private balconies, massive TVs, and complimentary local car service.

Burbank

Holiday Inn Burbank-Media Center

150 E Angeleno Avenue; tel: 818-841 4770; www.ihg.com; $$

Comfy chain option, with attractive rooms, panoramic views from the Crystal View Lounge on the 18th floor, heated outdoor pool, business center, and gym, plus free Wi-Fi and Bob Hope Airport (Burbank) shuttle.

Sheraton Universal Hotel

333 Universal Hollywood Drive, Universal City; tel: 818-980 1212; www. sheratonuniversal.com; $$$

Large, upscale rooms from the Sheraton stable, some with sweeping views of the Hollywood Hills; just five minutes from Universal Studios. Comes with outdoor terrace and pool (with private cabanas), huge fitness center, business center, and contemporary restaurant, Californias.

Little Ethiopia, Koreatown, and The Grove

Farmer's Daughter Hotel

115 S Fairfax Avenue; tel: 323-937 3930; www.farmersdaughterhotel.com; $$$

Conveniently located across from the Farmers' Market (naturally), this is a handsome rustic-chic property with free Wi-Fi and flat-screen TVs. Originally opened in the 1960s, it was remodeled in 1999 to tell the story of a young country girl through playful

Soaking up the rays at The Langham Huntington

design, handcrafted furnishings, and curated art (it was most recently renovated in 2017).

The Langham Huntington

1401 South Oak Knoll Avenue, Pasadena; tel: 626-568 3900, www.langhamhotels.com; $$$

A stunning, historic pastoral resort that opened in 1907, designed by Charles Whittlesey in the Spanish Mission Revival style, complete with Japanese gardens. It's been part of the luxury Langham portfolio since 2008, with spacious rooms dressed in classic, period style, the Chuan Spa, pool, The Royce Wood-Fired Steakhouse, and afternoon tea with Wedgwood specialty teas in tailor-made Langham Rose Wedgwood teaware.

Melrose, West Hollywood, and the Sunset Strip

Chateau Marmont

8221 Sunset Boulevard; tel: 323-656 1010; www.chateaumarmont.com; $$$$

This iconic hotel opened as an apartment building in 1929, modeled on the Gothic-style Château d'Amboise in France's Loire Valley (it was converted into a hotel in 1931). Owned by famed hotelier André Balazs since 1990, the Charmont has hosted all manner of celebrities from Greta Garbo to Robert De Niro (in 1982 John Belushi was found dead of a drug overdose in bungalow No. 3). Choose from 63 elegant rooms, cottages, and bungalows, the majority with full kitchens, sitting areas or living rooms, and balconies. Enjoy a heated outdoor pool, free Wi-Fi, and Baroque Bar Marmont.

Élan Hotel

8435 Beverly Boulevard; tel: 323-658 6663; www.elanhotel.com; $$$

Good-value boutique hotel with an elegant, contemporary theme located in a busy shopping zone just north of the Beverly Center mall. Free Wi-Fi, breakfast, and wine and cheese in the late afternoon. Also with fitness center and spa.

Mondrian Hotel

8440 Sunset Boulevard, West Hollywood; tel: 323-650 8999; www.morganshotelgroup.com; $$$$

Built as an apartment building in 1959, this trendy, celebrity-frequented hotel plays on scale and illusion and exudes Hollywood attitude. The minimalist chic rooms by Benjamin Noriega-Ortiz usually come with kitchens and provide VIP access to the SkyBar, an ivy-covered pavilion perched above the rooftop pool.

The Orlando

8384 W Third Street; tel: 323-658 6600; www.theorlando.com; $$$

Hip European-style boutique hotel with large rooms, a short walk from good restaurants and shopping areas,

Chateau Marmont

such as the Beverly Center, Third Street, and the Farmers' Market. Amenities include a heated saltwater swimming pool, fitness center, restaurant, and lounge.

The Standard

8300 Sunset Boulevard, West Hollywood; tel: 323-650 9090; www.standardhotels. com; $$$

One of the hippest hotels on the strip, with mid-century wavy Modern facade, bizarre deep blue Astroturf pool deck, and floor-to-ceiling shagged lobby. Rooms come with stylish, contemporary decor, free Wi-Fi, and mood lighting. The lobby features art videos and live performance, while 'top-top-secret' nightclub 'mmhmmm' (Sat 10pm–2am) and the desert-backdrop Cactus Lounge complete the picture.

Sunset Tower Hotel

8358 Sunset Boulevard, West Hollywood; tel: 323-654 7100; www.sunsettowerhotel. com; $$$$

Historic luxury hotel with landmark Art Deco facade, designed by architect Leland A. Bryant, and opened in 1931. Features luxurious rooms, pool and terrace with city views, and the celebrated Tower Bar and Restaurant.

Long Beach

Hotel Metropole

205 Crescent Avenue, Avalon, Catalina Island; tel: 800-541 8528; www.hotel-metropole.com; $$$

Located on the beachfront in the Metropole Market Place. Some of the rooms have ocean views, fireplaces, spas, and private balconies. Restaurant, rooftop sundeck, and Jacuzzi. Free Wi-Fi and complimentary breakfast.

The Queen Mary Hotel

1126 Queens Highway; tel: 877-342 0738; www.queenmary.com; $$

Formerly the world's largest passenger ship, this historic liner is now docked in the harbor and has been converted into a hotel. Rooms feature authentic polished wood paneling, the original 1930s artwork, Art Deco styling, and openable portholes. Several restaurants, bar, spa, and on-board shopping.

The "Dolly" Varden Hotel

335 Pacific Avenue; tel: 562-432 8950; www.thevardenhotel.com; $$

A 1920s building modernized with sleek white contemporary decor and cozy rooms with free Wi-Fi, flat-screen TVs, and boutique touches. The location, a block from Pine Avenue, also makes this a great choice.

Westin Long Beach

333 E Ocean Boulevard; tel: 562-436 3000; www.starwoodhotels.com; $$

Spacious rooms have full bay windows and ocean views. Located across from the Convention Center, with restaurant, bar, pool, fitness center, saunas, and business center.

Dining at Clifton's Cafeteria

RESTAURANTS

Like its entertainment industry, LA's restaurants are often as much about image as they are about cuisine. The most popular restaurants attract a steady clientele, inspire the hip and famous to clamor for a reservation, and try to provide a special something that can't be found at the next place.

With over 20,000 dining options, that 'special something' comes in the form of everything from fast-food shacks to star-rated formal affairs. Each is invariably frequented by colorful Angelenos doing their thing; in fact, waiting for a chili dog and fries with a virtual people zoo at Pink's sidewalk grubbery is as glamorous an experience as dining alfresco next to Angelina Jolie at glitzy Spago. Wherever you dine, it's bound to be fun.

Although restaurant decor and glitz are often appetizing enough to keep diners coming back, in recent years the dining experience has focused more on the food itself. With fantastic farm-fresh produce and superior fish and meats widely available through-out the state, today's 'California cuisine' reflects whatever's in season. The results are vibrant and creative preparations that are generously infused with influences from across the globe. Whether you crave sushi, French, Mexican, Burmese, Italian, vegetarian, or anything else imaginable, this town's got it and got it good.

Most areas have a range of restaurants to suit all budgets. Three of the most popular areas for dining out are West Hollywood, Beverly Hills, and Santa Monica; these are also the places where you will find the widest range of choices. Reservations are generally not required except in very prestigious or popular establishments.

Downtown LA

Clifton's Cafeteria

648 S Broadway; tel: 213-627 1673; www.cliftonsla.com; Tue–Thu 11am–9pm, Fri 11am–10pm, Sat 10am–10pm, Sun 10am–9pm; $$

Classic 1935 cafeteria with bizarre decor: giant faux redwood tree, waterfall, and stuffed grizzly. The food plays on traditional American snacks; jell-o in little jam cups, on top of cheesecake, plus corned beef and cabbage and the like. Look for Ray Bradbury's favorite booth, decorated with memorabilia.

Throughout this book, price guide for a two-course meal for one with an alcoholic drink:
$$$ = above US$50
$$ = US$25–50
$ = below US$25

Workaholic! sell their gourmet Korean fusion dumplings at Smorgasburg

Cole's Pacific Electric Buffet

118 E 6th Street; tel: 213-622 4090;
Mon–Wed & Sun 11am–midnight, Thu–Sat
11am–2am; $$

In the same spot since 1908, this is
LA's oldest restaurant. The decor and
food haven't changed much, and the
rich, hearty French-dip sandwiches are
still loaded with steak, pastrami, or
brisket – a dish supposedly invented
at this very spot, a claim challenged by
Philippe's.

Otium

222 S Hope Street; tel: 213-935 8500;
www.otiumla.com; Tue–Thu 11.30am–
2.30pm & 5.30–10pm, Fri 11.30am–2.30pm
& 5.30–11pm, Sat 10.30am–2.30pm &
5.30–11pm, Sun 10.30am–2.30pm &
5.30–10pm; $$$

Trendy restaurant from chef Tim Holl-
ingsworth, featuring a terrace opposite
The Broad lined with olive trees. Expect
contemporary American dishes such as
foie-gras funnel cake with strawberries,
and big fin squid.

The Palm

1100 S Flower Street; tel: 213-763
4600; www.thepalm.com/restaurants/
los-angeles; Mon–Thu 11.30am–10pm,
Fri 11.30am–11pm, Sat 5–11pm, Sun
5–9.30pm; $$$

From the perfect steaks to the Nova
Scotia lobsters flown in daily, the clas-
sic American food is impeccable at
this acclaimed Northern Italian steak-
house in a historic toy factory. The first
Palm opened in New York in 1926,
and it has since grown into a mini-
chain.

Redbird

114 E 2nd Street; tel: 213-788 1191;
www.redbird.la; Mon–Thu 5–10pm,
Fri 11.30am–2pm & 5–11pm, Sat
10am–2pm & 5–11pm, Sun 10am–2pm &
5–10pm; $$$

Chef Neal Fraser's innovative, contemporary American cuisine is served
in the beautifully converted 1885 rec-
tory of the old Cathedral of Saint Vibi-
ana. Dishes might include chicken pot
pie, sensational barbecue smoked
tofu, and rainbow curried carrots, as
well as plenty of fresh fish.

Smorgasburg

Alameda Produce Market, 785 Bay Street;
tel: 718-928 6603; http://la.smorgasburg.
com; Sun 10am–4pm; $

The hip weekly Williamsburg (New
York) food market now has a branch
in LA, with around 100 delectable
stands such as Black Sugar Ribs
Co, Burritos La Palma, Donut Friend,
Sticky Rice on Wheels, and TJ's Tacos.
Arrive hungry.

Sugarfish

600 W 7th Street; tel: 213-627 3000;
https://sugarfishsushi.com; Mon–Sat
11.30am–10pm, Sun noon–9pm; $$

Cult LA sushi chain, with Chef Noza-
wa's offerings reasonably priced (for
LA), with sets ranging from $19–27 and

Water Grill shrimp salad

fish sourced from local markets daily. Guests are seated on a first come, first-served basis only.

Water Grill

544 S Grand Avenue; tel: 213-891 0900; www.watergrill.com; Mon–Thu 11.30am–10pm, Fri 11.30am–11pm, Sat 5–11pm, Sun 4–10pm; $$$

One of the top-priced, top-notch spots for munching on California cuisine, with the focus on seafood, prepared in all manner of colorful ways – such as mint bass ceviche, or big-eye tuna with pomegranate couscous.

Silver Lake

Intelligentsia

3922 W Sunset Boulevard, Silver Lake; tel: 323-663 6173; www.intelligentsiacoffee. com; Sun–Wed 6am–8pm, Thu–Sat 6am–10pm; $

Coffee connoisseurs should make the trip to the king of LA's café scene, where top blends are fresh-roasted daily in vintage German roasters.

Hollywood

25 Degrees

7000 Hollywood Boulevard (Hollywood Roosevelt Hotel); tel: 323-785 7244; daily 24hr; $

The top gourmet burger joint in town, where you can pack your homemade burger with fried eggs, avocado, prosciutto, pesto, and even artisan cheeses, along with more traditional toppings.

Cactus Taqueria

950 Vine Street; tel: 323-464 5865; Sun–Thu 8am–3am, Fri & Sat 8am–4am; $

This tiny shack on the corner is a good spot to keep the evening going while you're club-hopping, with delicious quesadillas and burritos – and the best fish tacos in Hollywood. Cash only.

Griddle Café

7916 Sunset Boulevard; tel: 323-874 0377; www.thegriddlecafe.com; Mon–Fri 7am–4pm, Sat & Sun 8am–4pm; $$

The postmodern Hollywood version of a diner, where the pancakes, chili, and omelets come with various outlandish toppings (Oreos, breakfast cereal, etc), and the cheesecake French toast will make you cheer.

The Hungry Cat

1535 N Vine Street; tel: 323-462 2155; www.thehungrycat.com; Mon–Wed noon–10pm, Thu–Fri noon–11pm, Sat 11am–11pm, Sun 11am–10pm; $$

An outstanding raw bar with creatively cooked seafood dishes in a sleek and modern (but lively) setting, with top-notch cocktails to boot.

Moun of Tunis

7445 Sunset Boulevard; tel: 323-874 3333; www.mounoftunis.la; daily 5–11pm; $$

Mouth-watering Tunisian and Moroccan food presented in huge, multi-course meals, heavy on the spices and rich on the exotic flavors – plus regular belly dancing.

Intelligentsia coffee shop

Off Vine

6263 Leland Way; tel: 323-962 1900; www.
offvine.com; daily 11.30am–10.30pm; $$$

Dine on eclectic California cuisine – Cornish game hen with cornbread, turkey breast with jalapeño relish – in a renovated but still authentic Craftsman bungalow from 1908.

Providence

5955 Melrose Avenue; tel: 323-460 4170;
www.providencela.com; Mon–Thu 6–10pm,
Fri noon–2pm & 6–10pm, Sat 5.30–10pm,
Sun 5.30–9pm; $$$

Near the top of the LA pricey-restaurant scene, and for good reason: the place is swarming with foodies, who come for the black sea bass, foie-gras ravioli, lump blue crab, and plenty of other tremendous choices crafted by chef Michael Cimarusti.

Roscoe's House of Chicken and Waffles

1514 N Gower Street; tel: 323-466 7453;
www.roscoeschickenandwaffles.com; Mon–
Thu 8.30am–midnight, Fri & Sat 8am–4am,
Sun 8am–midnight; $

This diner – a soul food restaurant chain founded in 1975 by Herb Hudson, a Harlem native – attracts all sorts for its fried chicken, greens, and thick waffles.

Venice, Santa Monica, and Malibu

Big Daddy's Pizza

1425 Ocean Front Walk, Venice; tel: 310-806 8486; www.bigdaddyspizzavenice.
com; daily 10am–9.30pm; $

Classic hole-in-the-wall on the boardwalk that's been an institution with local surfers and kids for years; grab one of the huge slices of pizza, lobster roll, or fried oreo on a stick, and munch on the beach.

Blue Star Donuts

1142 Abbot Kinney Boulevard, Venice; tel:
310-450 5630, www.bluestardonuts.com;
daily 7am (until they run out); $

Fabulous gourmet doughnuts at an outpost of the lauded Portland outfit, offering chic flavors such as lemon, poppy, and buttermilk, and blueberry, bourbon, and basil.

Cha Cha Chicken

1906 Ocean Avenue, Santa Monica; tel:
310-581 1684; www.chachachicken.
com; Mon–Fri 11am–10pm, Sat & Sun
10am–10pm; $

This no-frills Caribbean beach shack south of the pier is old-school Santa Monica, with excellent jerk chicken, cubano sandwiches, and fresh fruit juices.

Coast

1 Pico Boulevard (Shutters on the Beach),
Santa Monica; tel: 310-587 1707; www.
shuttersonthebeach.com; daily 7am–10pm;
$$$

This classy hotel restaurant is right on the beach, the perfect place to eat breakfast or just check out the board-

Fresh flowers decorate the dining table at Gjelina

walk scene with a chilled wine and guacamole dip.

Father's Office

1018 Montana Avenue, Santa Monica; tel: 310-736 2224; www.fathersoffice.com; Mon–Thu 5pm–1am, Fri 4pm–2am, Sat noon–2am, Sun noon–midnight; $$

If you're as interested in celebrity-spotting as in dinner, check out this chic gastropub, which opened back in 1953, where the craft beers and the chef Sang Yoon's 'Office Burger' have garnered a loyal following.

Gjelina

1429 Abbot Kinney Boulevard, Venice; tel: 310-450 1429; www.gjelina.com; daily 8am–midnight; $$$

Hip American bistro serving artful small plates like grilled octopus and grilled king oyster mushrooms, as well as pizzas and various charcuterie.

James' Beach

60 N Venice Boulevard, Venice; tel: 310-823 5396; www.jamesbeach.com; Mon & Tue 6pm–1.30am, Wed–Sun 11.30am–1.30am; $$$

Another Venice institution (it featured in the movie *I Love You Man* in 2009), known locally for its fresh mahi-mahi tacos; with its casual beach vibe not far from the boardwalk, it makes it a fun place for food, wine, or cocktails.

Rae's Restaurant

2901 Pico Boulevard, Santa Monica; tel: 310-828 7937; daily 5.30am–9pm; $

Classic diner dating from 1958, which serves heavy, tasty comfort food. Its turquoise-blue facade and interior have been seen in many movies, notably *True Romance*, Steve Martin's *Bowfinger*, and the 2004 remake of *Starsky and Hutch*. Cash only.

Umami Burger

525 Broadway, Santa Monica; tel: 310-451 1300; www.umamiburger.com; Mon–Thu 11am–11pm, Fri 11am–midnight, Sat 10.30am–midnight, Sun 10.30am–11pm; $

Home of the truffle burger, manly chick burger, maple bacon fries, and several other artful creations (including ahi tuna burger), this mini chain has become a major coast-to-coast fad.

Beverly Hills

Cut

9500 Wilshire Boulevard (Beverly Wilshire); tel: 310-276 8500; www.wolfgangpuck. com; Mon–Thu 6–10pm, Fri 6–11pm, Sat 5.30–11pm; $$$

This hotel steakhouse, with chef Wolfgang Puck at the helm, was designed by Richard Meier and looks like the Getty Center cafeteria. If you fancy a splurge on exquisite steaks that cost up to $100, Kobe short ribs, and Maine lobster, this is the place.

Il Fornaio

301 N Beverly Drive; tel: 310-550 8330; www.ilfornaio.com; Mon–Thu 7am–10pm, Fri 7am–11pm, Sat 7.30am–11pm, Sun

Bob's Big Boy diner

7.30am–10pm; $$$
A bustling and bright Italian trattoria with excellent breads, soups, pizzas, pastas, and rotisserie dishes and lively, crowded atmosphere. Also features a wood stove, mesquite grill, patio dining, and a bakery café. Reservations recommended.

Matsuhisa Beverly Hills

129 N La Cienega Boulevard; tel: 310-659 9639; https://matsuhisabeverlyhills.com; Mon–Fri 11.45am–2.15pm & 5.45–10.15pm, Sat & Sun 5.45–10.15pm; $$$
Nobu Matsuhisa's landmark restaurant is the biggest name in town for sushi, charging the highest prices. Essential if you're a raw-fish aficionado with a wad of cash.

Mr Chow

344 N Camden Drive; tel: 310-278 9911; www.mrchow.com; Mon–Fri noon–2.30pm & 6–11.30pm; Sat & Sun 6–11.30pm; $$$
Celebrity spotting generally accompanies excellent Beijing-style (multiple-dish) Chinese fare including duck, dumplings, lobster, and house-made garlic noodles. A modern, see-and-be-seen setting since 1974 (the original opened in London). Reservations recommended.

Bob's Big Boy

4211 W Riverside Drive; tel: 818-843 9334; www.bigboy.com; daily 24hr; $

The classic chain diner, fronted by the plump burger lad, and a veritable pop-architecture classic (1949), saved from demolition through the efforts of preservationists.

Don Cuco

218 E Orange Grove Avenue; tel: 818 955-8895; www.doncuco.com; Mon–Thu 11am–10pm, Fri–Sun 11am–11pm; $$
Top-notch quesadillas, spicy soups, burritos, and potent margaritas are the prime draws at this small Mexican restaurant, open since 1969.

Koreatown and The Grove

Dong Il Jang

3455 W 8th Street, Koreatown; tel: 213-383 5757; Tue–Sun 11.30am–10pm; $$
Cosy little Korean restaurant – one of K-Town's oldest – where the meat is cooked at your table and the food is consistently good, especially the grilled chicken, kimchi fried rice, and roasted gui prime rib. Tempura dishes and a sushi bar are added draws.

Du-par's

6333 W 3rd Street, The Grove; tel: 323-933 8446; www.dupars.net; daily 24hr; $$
A long-standing LA institution (since 1938), located in the Farmers' Market, which draws a whole host of old-timers for its gut-busting comfort food, from chicken pot pie to cheeseburgers to the beloved buttermilk hot cakes.

Soowon Galbi Korean BBQ

856 S Vermont Avenue, Koreatown; tel: 213-365 9292; http://soowongalbi.net; daily 11.30am–10.30pm; $$

Koreatown institution since 1986, specializing in the namesake beef short-rib dish, as well as pork belly and in-house kimchi. Use the tabletop grills to get the meats sizzling.

Taylor's Steak House

3361 W 8th Street, Koreatown; tel: 213-382 8449; www.taylorssteakhouse.com; Mon–Thu 11.30am–9.30pm, Fri 11.30am–10.30pm, Sat 4–10.30pm, Sun 4–9.30pm; $$$

Old-school steakhouse marooned in Koreatown but still serving the best slabs of meat in the city for the price; the prime top sirloin and the French onion soup are magnificent.

El Pueblo and Chinatown

Howlin' Ray's

727 N Broadway Avenue (Far East Plaza), Chinatown; tel: 213-935 8399; www.howlinrays.com; Tue–Fri 11am–7pm, Sat & Sun 10am–7pm; $

Nashville's signature spicy hot fried chicken sandwich arrived in LA in 2016 and instantly became a cult hit – expect long lines at this counter-only Chinatown mall diner.

La Luz del Dia

1 Olvera Street, El Pueblo; tel: 213-628 7495; www.luzdeldia.com; Mon 11am–3.30pm, Tue–Thu 10am–8pm, Fri & Sat 10am–9pm, Sun 8.30am–9pm; $$

Mexican restaurant that's been here since 1959, worth seeking out for its authentic Michoacán food, fiery tacos, tostadas, and combo plates, served in sizeable enough portions to make you sweat.

Phoenix Inn

301 Ord Street, Chinatown; tel: 213-629 2812; www.phoenixfood.us; daily 11am–1am; $$

Chinatown restaurant open since 1965 that offers an array of tasty noodle soups, hot pots, fried noodles, and tofu items. The seafood, duck, and sliced prime rib are also worth a try.

Pasadena

Dog Haus

105 N Hill Avenue; tel: 626-577 4287; www.doghaus.com; daily 11am–10pm; $

Excellent good-sized and generously built hot dogs and burgers with delicious toppings that will surely put a big smile on your face. This place is consistently busy and it can get really crowded at lunchtime.

Fair Oaks Pharmacy & Soda Fountain

1526 Mission Street, South Pasadena; tel: 626-799 1414; www.fairoakspharmacy.net; Mon–Sat 9am–9pm, Sun 10am–7pm; $

Restored soda fountain with many old-time drinks like lime rickeys, root beer floats, milkshakes, and egg creams – a

Jitlada restaurant is a Thai cult classic

historic 1915 highlight along the former Route 66.

Little Tokyo and the Arts District

Daikokuya
327 E 1st Street; tel: 213-626 1680; www.daikoku-ten.com; Mon–Thu 11am–midnight, Fri & Sat 11am–1am, Sun 11am–11pm; $
Credited with sparking the ramen craze in LA in 2002, this Japanese noodle house still knocks out delicious tonkotsu noodle bowls, with marinated pork belly, bamboo shoots, and hard-boiled eggs soaked in special sauce. No reservations.

Sushi Gen
422 E 2nd Street; tel: 213-617 0552; www.sushigen-dtla.com; Mon–Fri 11.15am–2pm & 5.30–9.30pm, Sat 5–9.30pm; $$
The melt-in-your-mouth toro and salmon understandably attract crowds of people to this gem of a sushi restaurant in Little Tokyo. Go at lunch to beat the crowds and take advantage of the reasonably priced lunch specials.

Wurstküche
800 E 3rd Street; tel: 213-687 4444; www.wurstkuche.com; daily 11am–1.30am; $
Arts District restaurant and contemporary German/Belgian-themed beer hall with a cult following, famed for its wide range of delicious sausages (with ingredients such as apples, yukon potatoes, and rubbed sage), and craft beers.

Los Feliz, Thai Town, and Little Armenia

Fred 62
1854 N Vermont Avenue, Los Feliz; tel: 323-667 0062; www.fred62.com; daily 24hr; $$
Designed like something out of the 1950s and on the way to Griffith Park, this diner offers stylish, affordable California-cuisine twists on familiar staples like salads, burgers, and fries, plus a tempting array of pancakes and omelets.

Jitlada
5233 Sunset Boulevard, Thai Town; tel: 323-667 9809; Tue–Sun 11am–3pm & 5–10.30pm; $
In a dreary mini-mall, but a cult favorite; the spicy chicken, squid, oxtail curry, papaya salad, and fishball and other seafood curries more than make up for the setting. Affordable prices, too.

Sanamluang Café
5176 Hollywood Boulevard, Thai Town; tel: 323-660 8006; daily 11am–3.30am; $
You can't beat the cheap, excellent, and plentiful noodles, or the squid salad and spicy shrimp soup, at this nearly all-night Thai place (try the classic tom kha kai).

Melrose, West Hollywood, and the Sunset Strip

Barney's Beanery
8447 Santa Monica Boulevard; tel: 323-654 2287; https://barneysbeanery.

Patronize Carney's for a novel dining experience

com; Mon–Fri 11am–2pm, Sat & Sun 9am–2am; $$

Hundreds of bottled beers and hot dogs, hamburgers, and classic bowls of chili, served in a hip, grungy environment since 1927. Angelenos can be divided up by those who love or hate the place – everyone knows it.

Bossa Nova

685 N Robertson Boulevard; tel: 310-657 5070; www.bossanovafood.com; Mon–Thu 11am–11.30pm, Fri & Sat 11am–3.30am, Sun 11am–midnight; $$

Enticing Brazilian restaurant with a menu that includes South American staples (shrimp croquettes, fried yucca, etc) and more unexpected items such as chicken skewers, filet mignon, and pasta.

Carney's

8351 Sunset Boulevard; tel: 323-654 8300; www.carneytrain.com; Sun–Thu 11am–midnight, Fri & Sat 11am–3am; $$

This renovated railcar has become something of an LA icon (featuring in the TV show *Entourage*) – though the food is standard diner fare (with especially good burgers and hot dogs), the novelty of eating in an old Pacific Railroad train makes a trip worthwhile.

Carlitos Gardel

7963 Melrose Avenue; tel: 323-655 0891; www.carlitosgardel.com; Mon–Thu & Sat 6–11pm, Fri 11.30am–2.30pm & 6–11pm, Sun 5–10pm; $$$

Seriously rich and tasty Argentine cuisine and specialty steaks – heavy on the beef and spices, with sausages and garlic adding to the kick.

Gracias Madre

8905 Melrose Avenue; tel: 323-978 2170; www.graciasmadreweho.com; Mon–Fri 11am–11pm, Sat & Sun 10am–11pm; $$

'Thankyou mother' specializes in organic, plant-based (vegan) Mexican-inspired food, with tasty mains ranging from black-bean burgers and enchiladas stuffed with zucchini, cashews, and avocado, to coconut ceviche tostada and grilled corn cakes.

Osteria Mozza

6602 Melrose Avenue; tel: 323-297 0100; www.osteriamozza.com; Mon–Fri 5.30–11pm, Sat 5–11pm, Sun 5–10pm; $$$

Italian fine-dining culinary star, with an amazing mozzarella bar showcasing handcrafted varieties from cream-filled burrata to spongy bufala.

Pink's Hot Dogs

709 N La Brea Avenue; tel: 323-931 7594; www.pinkshollywood.com; Mon–Thu & Sun 9.30am–2am, Fri & Sat 9.30am–3am; $

Depending on your taste, these monster hot dogs – topped with anything from bacon and chili cheese to pastrami and Swiss cheese – are lifesavers or gut bombs, served here since 1939.

World-famous Randy's Donuts

Urth Caffe

8565 Melrose Avenue; tel: 310-659 0628; www.urthcaffe.com; Sun–Thu 6am–11pm, Fri & Sat 6am–midnight; $

Popular café and casual lunch spot with organic coffee and tea. Healthy meals are on offer and there is a selection of delicious desserts, which are made in house. The outdoor patio is a well-known spot for celeb-spotting.

Long Beach

Alegria Cocina Latina

115 Pine Avenue; tel: 562-436 3388; www.alegriacocinalatina.com; Mon 5–10pm, Tue & Sun 11am–10pm, Thu & Fri 11am–2am, Sat 5pm–2am; $$

Tapas, gazpacho, and a variety of 'platos principales' served with sangría on the patio, and to the beat of live flamenco on weekends. Good location near the harbor in Downtown Long Beach.

Belmont Brewing Company

25 39th Place; tel: 562-433 3891; www.belmontbrewing.com; Mon–Thu 11.30am–10.30pm, Fri 11.30am–11.30pm, Sat 10am–11pm, Sun 10am–10.30pm; $$

Authentic brewery on the beach with a commanding view of the Long Beach skyline, Palos Verdes, and Catalina Island. Serves salads, sandwiches, pasta, meat, and fish entrées, and, of course, beer.

The Sky Room

40 S Locust Avenue; tel: 562-983 2703, www.theskyroom.com; Mon–Thu 5.30–10pm, Fri–Sat 5.30–11pm, Sun 4.30–9pm; $$$

First opened in 1926, this classy restaurant atop the Breakers Hotel transports diners to an earlier era of fine dining, dancing, and entertainment, with stunning Art Deco decor, California-French cuisine, romantic music, panoramic views over the ocean and city, and extensive wine list. Reservations recommended.

LAX (Inglewood)

Pann's

6710 La Tijera Boulevard, Inglewood; tel: 323-776 3770; www.panns.com; Mon–Sat 7am–3pm, Sun 8am–4pm, summer hours extended; $

Open since 1958 and one of the all-time great Googie diners – with a pitched roof, big neon sign, exotic plants, and wealth of primary colors – where you can't go wrong with the classic burgers or biscuits and gravy.

Randy's Donuts

805 W Manchester Avenue, Inglewood; tel: 310-645 4707; daily 24hr; $

This Pop Art fixture is hard to miss, thanks to the colossal doughnut sitting on the roof built in 1953 (memorably featured in *Iron Man 2*). Excellent for its signature piping-hot treats, which you can pick up at the drive-through on your way to or from LAX.

Broadner's bar

NIGHTLIFE

Nightlife in Los Angeles is world-famous, and it's not just for celebrities and Hollywood starlets. Everything from classic old-time bars and hopping nightclubs to sophisticated cocktail lounges and craft-beer joints is on offer.

Live music has always been part of the scene, from classical and folk to rock and hip-hop, while LA's comedy clubs are some of America's most famous. Downtown LA, including the Arts District, has definitely increased its nightlife appeal in recent years, though Hollywood, West Hollywood, the Sunset Strip, and Santa Monica remain the entertainment hotspots, with Koreatown, Silver Lake, and Echo Park the up-and-coming hipster neighborhoods.

The following listings are just a tiny selection. Note also that some landmark venues such as the Greek Theatre (see page 83), Musso & Frank Grill (see page 43), The Roxy (see page 92), TCL Chinese Theatre (see page 39), The Viper Room (see page 92), and Whisky-a-Go-Go (see page 90) are covered within the main routes section.

Bars

71Above
633 W 5th Street, 71st Floor, Downtown LA; tel: 213-712 2683; www.71above.com; Mon–Thu 11.30am–11pm, Fri 11.30am–midnight, Sat 5pm–midnight, Sun 5–10pm

This restaurant and sky lounge in US Bank Tower is the best place to view the city from above, whilst sampling carefully crafted seasonal cocktails conceived of, and named after, neighborhoods like Echo Park and Fairfax District.

Boardner's
1652 N Cherokee Avenue, Hollywood; tel: 323-462 9621; www.boardners.com; daily 4pm–2am

Former historic dive bar from 1942, now remodeled into sleek digs for tasteful drinking (and a decent happy hour). Also offers regular electronica, indie rock, and burlesque shows.

Drawing Room
1800 Hillhurst Avenue, Los Feliz; tel: 323-665 0135; daily 6am–2am

The quintessential, dingy, dark LA dive bar, this spot really does open at 6am every day of the year. It also offers free hot dogs and snacks, cheap drinks, jukebox, and a friendly local crowd. Cash only.

Dresden Room
1760 N Vermont Avenue, Los Feliz; tel: 323-665 4294; www.thedresden.com; Tue–Sat 5pm–2am, Sun & Mon 5pm–midnight

One of the neighborhood's classic bars and restaurants, perhaps best known for its 'Blood and Sand' whiskey cocktails and evening show (Tue–Sat

The Frolic Room   Jazz band playing the Kibitz Room

9pm–1.15am), in which the husband-and-wife lounge act of Marty and Elayne take requests from the crowd of old-timers and hipsters.

Formosa Café

7156 Santa Monica Boulevard, Hollywood; tel: 323-850 9050; www.theformosacafe.com; Mon–Sat 4pm–2am, Sun 10am–2am
Established in 1925 as a watering hole for Charlie Chaplin's adjacent United Artists studios, this creaky old spot is still alive with the ghosts of Bogie and Marilyn. Drink the potent spirits, but stay away from the average Chinese food.

Frolic Room

6245 Hollywood Boulevard; tel: 323-462 5890; daily 11am–2am
This classic LA bar (opened in 1930 inside the Pantages Theatre), decorated with Hirschfeld cartoons of celebrities, offers affordable drinks, cool jukebox, and a dark, authentic old-time ambience.

Joe Jost's

2803 E Anaheim Street, Long Beach; tel: 562-439 5446; www.joejosts.com; Mon–Sat 10am–11pm, Sun 10am–9pm
Most famous bar in Long Beach, open since 1924. Celebrated for its cheap drinks, basic sandwiches, English-style pickled eggs, and hot dogs.

Kibitz Room

419 N Fairfax Avenue; tel: 323-651 2030; www.cantersdeli.com/kibitz-room; daily 10.30am–1.40am

Attached to legendary 24-hour Canter's Deli, many rock legends have imbibed at this celebrated dive bar since 1961, which still offers cheap pours. Sunday is open-mic night, with live music and comedy offered the rest of the week.

The Rooftop at The Standard

550 S Flower Street, Downtown LA; tel: 213-892 8080; daily noon–10pm
The poseur pinnacle in Downtown LA, this is an alcohol-fuelled playpen where the silk-shirted-black-leather-pants crowd goes to hang in red metallic 'pods' with waterbeds and sprawl out on a rooftop Astroturf lawn.

Tiki Ti

4427 W Sunset Boulevard, Los Feliz; tel: 323-669 9381; www.tiki-ti.com; Wed–Sat 4pm–2am
This classic LA tiki bar (with just 12 stools, and a handful of tables against the walls), was founded by Ray Buhen in 1961, one of the original Filipino bartenders who worked for Tiki legend 'Don the Beachcomber', keeping his cocktail traditions alive (try the 'Blood and Sand' or 'Ray's Mistake').

The Walker Inn

3612 W 6th Street, Koreatown; tel: 213-263 2709; thewalkerinnla.com; daily 7pm–2am
Speakeasy-type bar with 'secret' door inside the Normandie Club (also a bar), offering craft cocktails served as part of the $70 Walker tasting menu (reservation required); normal tables are avail-

able on a walk-in basis (maximum 27 people in the bar at any time).

The Varnish

118 E 6th Street, Downtown LA; tel: 213-265 7089; www.thevarnishbar.com; daily 7pm–2am

Classic cocktail specialist, housed inside a refurbished storage room, hidden in the back of Cole's (see page 113) – it's not marked from the outside, but everyone knows it.

Nightclubs

The Abbey

692 N Robertson Boulevard, West Hollywood; tel: 310-289 8410; www.theabbeyweho.com; daily 11am–2am

World-famous gay bar, restaurant, nightclub, and host of LGBTQ events in the heart of WeHo that offers great people-watching, go-go dancers, and buzzing atmosphere.

Avalon Hollywood

1735 N Vine Street; tel: 323-462-8900; https://avalonhollywood.com; Fri 9.30pm–5am, Sat 9.30pm–7am

Major dance club spinning old-school favorites, along with the usual techno and house, with the occasional big-name DJ dropping in. Prices are among the most expensive in town.

Dirty Laundry

1725 N Hudson Avenue, Hollywood; tel: 323-462 6531; www.dirtylaundrybarla.com; Tue–Sat 10pm–2am

Fun bar and club (allegedly in Rudolph Valentino's former speakeasy) known for its inventive cocktails (bacon Manhattan slushy or almond old-fashioned anyone?) and 'hidden' entrance along an alley; ring the correct buzzer to get in.

La Cita

336 Hill Street, Downtown LA; tel: 213-687 7111; www.lacitabar.com; Mon–Fri 11am–2am, Sat & Sun 10am–2am

Classic Latino bar and dance club with outdoor patio (from 4pm) that attracts hordes of hipsters for its Punky Reggae Party on Friday and its Rockabilly Thursday happy hour (4–9pm).

The Virgil

4519 Santa Monica Boulevard; tel: 310-660 4540; www.thevirgil.com; daily 7pm–2am

This stylish bar and comedy club in East Hollywood transforms into a DJ showcase Thursday to Sunday, with a mash up of hits, hip-hop, and house.

Live music venues

Catalina Bar & Grill

6725 Hollywood Boulevard, Hollywood; tel: 323-466 2210; www.catalinajazzclub.com; Tue–Sun 6.30pm–midnight

A jazz institution with plenty of style and atmosphere, also serving meals and potent drinks. Originally a restaurant, until Dizzy Gillespie did a spot here in 1987.

The Echo

1822 Sunset Boulevard, Echo Park; tel:

The Comedy Store is LA's leading comedy venue

213-413 8200, www.spacelandpresents.com/events/the-echo; hours vary
Club with indie-rock bands playing in a dark, intense little hole for a crowd of serious hipsters. A good place to catch what's bubbling up on the underground music scene; morphs into hip dance club on Friday and Saturday nights.

Harvelle's
1432 4th Street, Santa Monica; tel: 310-395 1676; www.harvelles.com; daily 8pm–2am
A stellar blues joint near the Third Street Promenade, open since 1931, offering different performers nightly and a little funk, R&B, and burlesque thrown in too.

Hollywood Palladium
6215 Sunset Boulevard, Hollywood; tel: 323-962 7600; www.hollywoodpalladium.com; hours vary
Once a big-band dance hall, with an authentic 1940s interior, now home to all manner of hard rock, punk, and rap outfits.

Hotel Café
1623 N Cahuenga Boulevard, Hollywood; tel: 323-461 2040; www.hotelcafe.com; hours vary
Comfortable spot for acoustic acts and singer-songsmiths, as well as indie bands. Usually has the best line-up in town for this sort of thing, with two stages. Shows daily, usually from 7pm.

The Shrine Auditorium
665 W Jefferson Boulevard, South LA; tel: 213-748 5116; www.shrineauditorium.com; hours vary
Huge, 1926 Moorish curiosity that hosts touring pop acts, choral gospel groups, and countless award shows.

The Troubadour
9081 Santa Monica Boulevard, West Hollywood; tel: 310-276 6168; www.troubadour.com; hours vary
An old 1957 mainstay that's been through a lot of incarnations in its 60-plus years. Today it sees mostly various flavors of indie rock.

Comedy clubs

The Comedy Store
8433 W Sunset Boulevard, West LA; tel: 323-656 6228; https://thecomedystore.com; daily 7pm–2.30am
LA's premier comedy showcase, and popular enough to be spread over three rooms – which means there's usually space, even on weekends. Two drink minimum.

Groundlings
7307 Melrose Avenue, West LA; tel: 323-934 4747; www.groundlings.com; shows usually Mon–Sat 8pm and Sun 7.30pm
Pioneering venue where only the gifted survive (Melissa McCarthy and Kristen Wiig among them), with furious improv events and high-wire comedy acts that can inspire greatness or groans. No alcohol.

Hard cash

A–Z

A

Age restrictions

The legal age to drink alcohol in Los Angeles is 21 (as in the rest of the country); be sure to carry photo identification. Recreational marijuana sales are legal in California for 21s and over, but the rules are fairly strict. While Californians can drive at 16, most car-rental companies only allow drivers aged 21 and above.

B

Budgeting

The prices listed below are approximate.

Airport transfer. To Downtown: taxi $46.50, Super Shuttle $17.

Bus and Metro fares. $1.75 base fare, 50¢ transfers. Specials: $7 day-pass; $25 weekly pass.

Car rental. Prices vary greatly. Count on $35–$50 per day with unlimited mileage.

Discount cards. The Go Los Angeles Card provides up to 50 percent discount on admission to major attractions (starting at $85 for one day). For most visitors, the card will only save you money if you buy a 3- or 5-day card and visit all the major attractions.

Hotels. Double room, per night (14 percent tax not included): top-end $210 and up; moderate $110–$210; budget under $110.

Meals and drinks. Main course at a budget restaurant $8–15; moderate $12–25; fine-dining establishment $25–40. For drinks, beers usually cost $6–9, and a glass of house wine $6–15.

Parking lots (car parks). $2–$6 per hour; many have a maximum $5–$6 charge; Downtown ramps and hotel parking $12–$30 per day.

C

Children

With its theme parks, movie-related attractions, and child-friendly restaurants, Los Angeles is an incredibly exciting place for kids. Museums and sights usually come with a children's discount.

Clothing

Bring comfortable, casual clothes and shoes. In January and February you might also want to pack clothes suitable for rainy weather. Formal restaurants may require a jacket and tie for men and smart clothes for women; otherwise, casual chic is the usual attire.

Consulates

Many countries maintain consulates or have overseas representatives in

LAX, Los Angeles' airport   *Children learning to surf*

Los Angeles. Official embassies are in Washington, D.C.

Australia: 2029 Century Park E; tel: 310-229 2300; www.losangeles.con sulate.gov.au.

Canada: 550 S Hope Street, 9th Floor; tel: 213-346 2700; www.losangeles. gc.ca.

United Kingdom: 2029 Century Park E, Suite 1350; tel: 310-789 0031; www. gov.uk/government/world/usa.

Crime and safety

Travelers should take the normal precautions; carry bags and purses closed and across your body, keep wallets in front – not back – pockets, and don't flash money around. You should also keep a firm grip on your phone/iPod/tablet on the Metro (these are occasionally snatched just as the doors close). Mugging can and does happen, but rarely during the day. Avoid wandering empty streets or the subway late at night (especially alone). The all-purpose emergency telephone number is **911**.

Customs regulations

There is no limit on the amount of money that you may bring in or take out of the US. However, you must declare amounts exceeding $10,000 or the foreign currency equivalent. Adult visitors may bring the following into the country duty free: 1 liter of alcohol, 200 cigarettes or 100 cigars; and gifts valued under $100.

Prohibited goods include: dangerous drugs, obscene publications, hazardous articles (eg fireworks), and narcotics. Travelers using medicines should carry a prescription and/or a note from their doctor and only the quantity required for their stay. Many food products are prohibited.

D

Disabled travelers

Many LA hotels have rooms with accessible features as well as wheelchair-accessible transportation and recreational amenities. TDD telephone lines are available for the hearing impaired. Contact the California Relay Service for the Hearing Impaired at 711 or: (Voice) 800-735 2922, (TDD/TTY) 800-735 2929. Most buses are equipped either with automatic wheelchair lifts, or, in the newer buses, low-floor access. You can contact the Metro Wheelchair Lift Hotline (800-621 7828). Many LA attractions and theme parks are set up to accommodate those with disabilities: visit the relevant websites for details.

E

Electricity

Throughout the United States the standard is 110–120 volts, 60 cycle AC. Plugs usually have two flat prongs. Overseas visitors without dual-voltage travel appliances will need a transformer and adapter plug.

Emergencies

For police, ambulance, or fire services dial: 911.

F

Festivals

Tournament of Roses. Pasadena's New Year's Day Tournament of Roses Parade attracts more than a million visitors to watch its marching bands and elaborate flower-emblazoned floats. www.tournamentofroses.com.

Mardi Gras. February. Floats, parades, costumes, and lots of singing and dancing at this Latin fun-fest, with traditional ceremonies on Olvera Street, Downtown, and campy antics in West Hollywood.

The Academy Awards. Late February/early March. Presented at a star-studded ceremony in the Dolby Theatre. Bleacher seats (free) are available on the red carpet (advanced reservation in around September). www.oscars.org.

Long Beach Grand Prix. April. Some of auto-racing's best drivers and souped-up vehicles zoom around Shoreline Drive. https://gplb.com.

Cinco de Mayo (May 5). Spirited parade (commemorating Mexico's defeat of the French at the Battle of Puebla, on May 5, 1862), along Olvera Street. There are also celebrations in most LA parks.

LA Pride. Mid-June. Parade on Santa Monica Boulevard in West Hollywood. Carnival atmosphere, hundreds of vendors, and an all-male drag football cheerleading team. https://lapride.org.

Lotus Festival. July. Echo Park celebration featuring Asian-Pacific food, music and, of course, the resplendent lotus blooms around Echo Park Lake. www.laparks.org/lotusfestival.

International Surf Festival. Early August. Three-day surf spectacular plus volleyball games, lifeguard races, sand soccer, and sandcastle design. www.surffestival.org.

Long Beach Jazz Festival. Mid-August. Famous and local jazz performers. www.longbeachjazzfestival.com.

New Blues Festival. September. Hear top blues performers at this annual event in Long Beach. www.newbluesfestival.com.

Halloween. October 31. A wild parade in West Hollywood, with all manner of bizarre outfits and characters on display. Or you can opt for the Halloween-themed events on the *Queen Mary* in Long Beach.

Dia de los Muertos. November 2. The 'Day of the Dead,' celebrated authentically throughout East LA and more blandly for tourists on Olvera Street. Mexican traditions, such as picnicking on the family burial spot and making skeleton puppets, are faithfully upheld.

Hollywood Christmas Parade. Last weekend in November. The first and best of the many Yuletide events, with a cavalcade of mind-boggling floats,

Docked at the Marina del Rey

marching bands, and famous and quasi-famous names from film and TV. www.thehollywoodchristmasparade.org.

Holiday Boat Parade. Early December. Marina del Rey is the site for this ocean-going display of brightly lit watercraft, supposedly the largest boat parade in the West. https://mdrboatparade.org.

H

Health

No vaccinations are required or recommended, unless you are arriving from an area with cholera or yellow fever. The only health hazards in LA are sunburn and heat exhaustion, especially in mid-summer.

Clinics and hospitals

If you do need medical assistance speak to the reception staff at your hotel; call 911 in an emergency (should you be in a serious accident don't worry, an ambulance will pick you up and charge later – at least $1,500). The LA area has several 'urgent care' walk-in clinics. Try the Hollywood Walk-In Clinic (www.hollywoodclinic.net), or Downtown Urgent Care (www.downtownlosangelesurgentcare.com). If you need serious medical attention, contact any of the major hospitals, most of which have 24-hour emergency (trauma) rooms. These include: Providence Saint John's Health Center (2121 Santa Monica Boulevard; Santa Monica; tel: 310-829 5511; http://california.providence.org/saint-johns); Cedars-Sinai Medical Center (8700 Beverly Boulevard; tel: 800-233 2771; www.cedars-sinai.edu); and Hollywood Presbyterian Medical Center (1300 N Vermont Avenue; tel: 213-413 3000; www.hollywoodpresbyterian.com).

Insurance

The US operates a private healthcare system and if you do get sick or have an accident, things can get incredibly expensive; organize travel insurance before your trip, just in case. Emergency treatment is generally excellent, but note that even basic care at a hospital emergency room can rise from $300 to $15,000 incredibly fast.

Pharmacies

Always bring enough prescription medicine from home to cover the length of your trip. For over-the-counter medicines go to Walgreens (many open 24hr; 1501 Vine Street in Hollywood) or Rite Aid (the branch in West Hollywood is open 24hr).

Hours and holidays

Department stores and shopping malls are generally open 10am–9pm on weekdays, 10am–6 or 7pm on Saturday, and 11am–5 or 6pm on Sunday. Individual stores are generally open Monday–Saturday from 9 or

LA has a vibrant LGBTQ community

10am to 5.30 or 6pm. In trendy shopping areas such as Melrose Avenue, stores often stay open until 11pm. Most museums are closed on Monday or one other day of the week. Banks are generally open Monday–Friday or Saturday 9am–5 or 6pm. When certain holidays (such as Christmas) fall on a Sunday, banks, post offices, and most stores close on the following Monday. They close on Friday if those holidays fall on a Saturday.

Public holidays
New Year's Day January 1
Martin Luther King Jr. Day Third Monday in January
Presidents' Day Third Monday in February
Memorial Day Last Monday in May
Independence Day July 4
Labor Day First Monday in September
Columbus Day Second Monday in October
Veterans' Day November 11
Thanksgiving Fourth Thursday in November
Christmas December 25

I

Internet

Wireless is king in Los Angeles, with free Wi-Fi hotspots throughout the city, complimentary connections at cafés like Starbucks, and most hotels offering it for no charge. Alternatively, stop by a branch of the LA Public Library, where free Wi-Fi and computer Internet access are available.

L

LGBTQ travelers

West Hollywood ('WeHo') is the center of LGBTQ life in LA. The magazine *Frontiers* (www.frontiersmedia.com) offers information on local LGBTQ events, arts, and entertainment. The annual LGBTQ Film Festival, Outfest (www.outfest.org), is a popular event. For more information, you can also contact the Los Angeles LGBT Center (https://lalgbtcenter.org), the world's largest provider of LGBTQ services. The center has six branches in the city. Same-sex marriage was legalized throughout the US in June 2015.

M

Media

Television and radio
Most hotel rooms have TVs and many have radio. The nationwide commercial networks are CBS, 4 ABC, 7 ABC, and Fox. Channel 28 (KCET) is a non-commercial educational, independent television channel. Many hotels also offer a range of cable-TV programs.

Newspapers and magazines.
The *Los Angeles Times* (www.latimes.com) is LA's main daily newspaper. *Los Angeles Magazine* (www.lamag.com), published monthly, has interesting fea-

Newspaper boxes　　　　　　　　　　　　　*Terminal Annex*

tures about LA life and excellent listings. A number of weekly and monthly publications are also good sources of information. They include the *LA Weekly* (www.laweekly.com) and the *Downtown News* (www.ladowntownnews.com). Foreign newspapers and magazines are sold at large newsstands, and at Book Soup bookstore (see page 92).

Money

Currency

The dollar ($) is divided into 100 cents (¢). Banknotes: $1, $2 (uncommon), $5, $10, $20, $50, and $100. Coins: 1¢ (known as a penny), 5¢ (nickel), 10¢ (dime), 25¢ (quarter), 50¢ (half dollar, less common). Dollar coins exist but are rarely encountered.

Banks and currency exchange

Banks are generally open 9am–5 or 6pm Monday–Friday or Saturday. Other foreign-exchange outlets include World Banknotes Exchange, Downtown at 520 S Grand Avenue, Suite L100 (tel: 213-627 5404; www.wbxchange.com) and Travelex, 8901 Santa Monica Boulevard inside US Bank (tel: 310-659 6093; www.travelex.com).

ATMs

Most people on vacation withdraw cash as needed from ATMs, which are at any bank branch and at many convenience stores and delis in the city, though the latter can charge fees of up to $3 for the service (in addition to bank charges).

Credit cards

Major credit cards (American Express, MasterCard, and Visa) are accepted in most hotels, stores, and restaurants (and are almost always required when you check-in at a hotel). You may be asked for supplementary identification.

Tipping

You should add 18–20 percent to restaurant and bar checks. Movie theater/theater ushers are not tipped, but doormen who provide a service (calling a cab, etc) and cloak-room attendants should be given no less than one dollar. Tip the parking valet when your car is brought to you. Hotel bell-hops should get $1–$2 per bag, and leaving hotel housekeeping $1–$2 per day, or $7–$15 per week, is expected. Tip taxi drivers about 15 percent.

Taxes

A sales tax of 9.5 percent is added to most purchases and restaurant checks in Los Angeles; it's 10.25 percent in Long Beach.

P

Postal service

The US Postal Service deals only with mail. Post offices are generally open 8.30 or 9am–5pm Monday to Friday, and some are open 9am–noon or later on Saturday. You can usually purchase stamps at the front desk in your hotel

Passengers at Union Station

and at drugstores and grocery stores. Letters can usually be mailed from major hotels, or dropped in one of the blue mailboxes located throughout the city. For more information, visit www.usps.com.

S

Smoking

Smoking is banned in Los Angeles restaurants and bars, although trendy spots have a tendency to ignore the rules; fines start at $100, but the onus is on the owner. Smoking is prohibited in most public spaces.

T

Telephones

Public telephones are becoming harder to find due to the popularity of cell phones. For overseas calls, purchase a prepaid calling card ($5, $10, and $20), which you can buy at most grocery stores and newsstands. For information (directory assistance) dial 411. The Greater Los Angeles area uses four different area codes.

Cell (mobile) phones

Travelers should check with their phone provider before travel to ensure their model will work in the US, and what the call charges will be. Even if your phone does work you'll need to be extra careful about roaming charges. If you intend to use your phone a lot, it can be much cheaper to buy a US SIM card ($10 or less); AT&T (www.att.com) is your best bet. Some networks (such as Verizon Wireless) also sell basic flip phones (with minutes) for as little as $25 (no paperwork or ID required).

International calls

To make an international call, dial the international access code (in the US it's 011), then the destination's country code, before the rest of the number. Note that the initial zero is omitted from the area code when dialing the UK, Ireland, Australia, and New Zealand from abroad.

Time zones

Los Angeles is in the Pacific time zone, 8 hours behind GMT. From the second Sunday in March to the first Sunday in November, the clock is advanced 1 hour for Daylight Saving Time (GMT minus 7 hours).

Tourist information

The LA Tourism & Convention Board (www.discoverlosangeles.com) operates four visitor centers: at the Inter-Continental Los Angeles Downtown, 900 Wilshire Boulevard in Downtown LA (daily 9am–8pm); San Pedro/Los Angeles Waterfront, 390 W 7th Street, San Pedro (Mon–Fri 9am–5pm); Union Station, 800 N Alameda Street (daily 9am–5pm); and at the Hollywood & Highland Center, 6801 Hollywood

Los Angeles Metro Red Line train at Hollywood/Vine station

Boulevard in Hollywood (Mon–Sat 9am–10pm, Sun 10am–7pm; tel: 323-467 6412). The Beverly Hills Visitor Center is at 9400 S Santa Monica Boulevard (Mon–Fri 9am–5pm, Sat & Sun 10am–5pm; tel: 310-248 1015, www.lovebeverlyhills.com). Santa Monica's Visitor Information Kiosk is at 1400 Ocean Avenue (daily 9am–5pm; tel: 310-393 0410, www.santamonica. com). The main visitor center is at 2427 Main Street (Mon–Fri 9am–5.30pm and Sat & Sun 9am–5pm; tel: 310-393 7593).

Transportation

Arrival

By air from North America: Direct flights connect many American and Canadian cities to Los Angeles. Special fares are available on these competitive routes. Fly-drive vacations, including flight, hotel, and rental car, are offered by many airlines.

International flights: All the major international carriers have either direct or one-stop flights to Los Angeles from Europe and the main Pacific airports.

By rail: Amtrak is America's passenger railroad company. LA's Amtrak terminal is located on the north side of Downtown at Union Station, 800 North Alameda Avenue. You can travel nationwide from here. For information call 1-800-872 7245; www.amtrak.com.

By bus: The main Greyhound bus terminal for long-distance travel is located in a seedy section of Downtown at 1716

E 7th Street; take a taxi. For additional information, call 213-629 8401 or 1-800-231 2222; www.greyhound. com. Mega Bus and Bolt Bus (both with frequent service to Las Vegas, Oakland, and San Francisco) use Patsaouras Transit Plaza, at Union Station.

Airports

Los Angeles International Airport (LAX) is the major international airport for southwestern California and lies 16 miles (26km) southwest of Downtown LA (tel: 310-646 5252; www.lawa. org). Among the modes of transportation available at LAX are an airport bus service, door-to-door shuttle van service, local bus lines, rental cars, and taxicabs.

If you're arriving from elsewhere in the US or from Mexico, you may also land at one of the regional airports in the LA area, such as Hollywood Burbank Airport (tel: 818-840 8840; www.bob hopeairport.com), Long Beach Airport (tel: 562-570 2619; www.lgb.org), or John Wayne Airport (tel: 949-252 5200; www.ocair.com).

Transportation within Los Angeles

The bulk of LA's public transportation is operated by the LA County Metropolitan Transit Authority (MTA or 'Metro').

Metrorail. LA's Metrorail (www.metro. net) subway and light-rail system encompasses six major lines, though extensions are planned in coming years. Trains run daily from 5am to midnight

LA bus

(2am Fri & Sat), about every 5mins during peak hours and every 10–15mins at other times. Fares (standard $1.75 one-way; day-passes $7; seven-days $25) must be loaded on a TAP stored-value card ($1); purchase your fare before you board at self-service machines.

Metrolink. Metrolink commuter trains (tel: 800-371 5465, www.metrolinktrains.com) ply primarily suburban-to-Downtown routes on weekdays. One-way fares range from $3.50–16.75.

MTA buses. Although initially bewildering, the MTA bus network (www.metro.net) is actually quite simple: the main routes run east–west and north–south. Buses on the major arteries between Downtown and the coast run roughly every 15–25min, 5am–2am; other routes, and the all-night services, are less frequent. Pay for a single ride with cash using exact change or a TAP stored-value card (standard fare $1.75 one-way; express buses and those taking a freeway usually $2.50). A seven-day pass is $25, also valid on the Metro.

Other buses. DASH buses operate through the LA Department of Transportation (LADOT; www.ladottransit.com), with a flat fare of 50¢ (or 35¢ using TAP card) for broad coverage throughout Downtown and limited routes elsewhere in the city. LADOT also operates quick, limited-stop routes called commuter express ($1.50–4.25 depending on distance).

Other local bus services include those for Orange County (www.octa.net), Long Beach (www.lbtransit.org), Culver City (www.culvercity.org/bus), and Santa Monica (www.bigbluebus.com).

Taxis. Cabs are plentiful throughout the Los Angeles area, but they are not cheap and you'll usually need to phone in advance for pick-up. Your hotel can do this for you. Reputable companies include LA Checker Cab (tel: 800-300 5007, www.ineedtaxi.com) and Yellow Cab (tel: 424-222 2222, https://layellowcab.com). Smartphone app services like Uber (www.uber.com) and Lyft (www.lyft.com) may prove less expensive.

Car rental. Renting a car is the traditional way to explore Greater Los Angeles, especially if you have a family. However, traffic is bumper-to-bumper much of the day (be sure to avoid rush hour) and improvements in public transportation are finally starting to challenge the belief that car is king.

Most rental agencies require you to be 21 years old (sometimes 25), have a valid driver's license, and a major credit card to rent a vehicle. Foreign travelers can use the license issued in their home country. Rental offices are located at the airports, Downtown locations, and even at some hotels, though it is normally cheaper to arrange car rental in advance. Major car rental firms include Enterprise (tel: 800-261 7331; www.enterprise.com), Dollar (tel: 800-800 4000;

Traffic in LA can get very congested

www.dollar.com), Hertz (tel: 800-654 3131; www.hertz.com), and National (tel: 800-222 9058; www.nationalcar.com). Rates vary on an almost daily basis, so it pays to shop around.

Insurance is usually optional, but non-US residents should buy it since their regular insurance might not be sufficient. Be sure to check that your car-rental agreement includes a Loss Damage Waiver (LDW). US drivers can normally use their personal car insurance to cover a rental vehicle.

Driving in LA

Drive on the right; pass (overtake) on the left. Unless there's a sign to the contrary, you can turn right on a red signal, providing you make a complete stop and check for pedestrians and traffic. Seat belts are mandatory; children under 8 must be in a child's car seat (in the back) unless they are 4ft 9ins (148 cm). Pedestrians have right-of-way at crosswalks. It is an offense to pass a school bus on a two-lane road when it is taking on or discharging passengers. Strict drink-driving laws are enforced.

Speed limits. If there are no posted speed limit signs, the maximum speed is 25mph (40km/h), and 55mph (90km/h) on freeways. Outside city limits, the limit on Interstate highways is 65mph (100km/h) with several 70mph (112km/h) segments.

Parking. LA has an abundance of parking restrictions, which are posted along the street. LA's parking lots (car parks) may be expensive for short-term stays but are cheaper than fines.

Gas stations. Most service stations stay open in the evening and on Sunday. Most are self-service. If you have a credit card you can generally pay at the pump. Otherwise, go inside and pay to activate the pump; you get a refund if you overpay. There are several grades of gasoline (petrol): regular unleaded (the cheapest) will suffice for most rental cars.

Visas and passports

Under the Visa Waiver Program, citizens of Australia, Ireland, New Zealand, and the UK do not require visas for visits of 90 days or less. You will, however, need to obtain Electronic System for Travel Authorization (ESTA) online before you fly ($14) via the official US Customs and Border Protection website. Canadians require a passport to cross the border, but can travel in the US for up to a year without a visa or visa waiver.

W

Weights and measures

The United States still uses the Imperial system, where things are measured in miles, feet, inches, gallons, and ounces and pounds. Temperature is measured in Fahrenheit, not Centigrade/Celsius.

Laura Harring in Mulholland Drive

BOOKS AND FILM

LA has attracted numerous literary talents over the years, from Charles Bukowski, F. Scott Fitzgerald, and Nathanael West, to Raymond Chandler and Ray Bradbury, though much of its creativity has been absorbed by the Hollywood movie industry. Since its inception, the list of movies set in California, and especially Los Angeles, has become endless. What follows provides just a taster.

Books

Fiction
Ask the Dust, by John Fante. The first and best of Fante's stories of itinerant poet Arturo Bandini, whose wanderings during the Depression highlight Los Angeles' faded glory and struggling residents.

The Big Sleep, by Raymond Chandler. Set in LA, this is Chandler's first novel to feature detective Philip Marlowe.

The Last Tycoon, by F. Scott Fitzgerald. The legendary author's unfinished final work on the power and glory of Hollywood.

Post Office, by Charles Bukowski. An alcohol- and sex-soaked romp through some of LA's more festering back alleys, with a mailman surrogate for Bukowski as your guide. One of several Bukowski books exploring the city's dark side.

The Day of the Locust, by Nathanael West. The best book about LA not involving detectives: an apocalyptic story of the fringe characters at the edge of the film industry, which culminates in a glorious riot and utter chaos.

Non-fiction
City of Quartz, by Mike Davis. The most important modern history of LA, in this case from a leftist perspective, vividly covering cops, riots, politicians, movies, and architecture.

Film

The Artist, 2011. Showered with awards galore (including an Oscar for Best Picture), this exceptional romantic comedy-drama traces Hollywood's last days of silent films through the relationship of a fading silent-movie actor and an early 'talkies' starlet.

Beverly Hills Cop, 1984. Eddie Murphy plays a wise-cracking Detroit cop who comes to Beverly Hills to solve the murder of his best friend.

The Big Lebowski, 1998. The quintessential Angeleno, Jeff Bridges is 'The Dude' in this cult movie by Joel and Ethan Coen, an LA slacker who gets attacked by a pair of thugs mistaking him for a millionaire.

Boyz N the Hood, 1991. Landmark movie that cemented the LA stereotype as a land of gangs and guns, starring Cuba Gooding Jr in his first big role, and Lawrence Fishburne as his dad.

Chinatown, 1974. Jack Nicholson hunts down corruption in this dark crit-

Emma Stone and Ryan Gosling in multi-award winning La La Land

icism of the forces that animate the town: venal politicians, black-hearted land barons, crooked cops, and a morally neutered populace; an essential movie about LA.

Clueless, 1995. Perhaps the most quotable teen movie of all time, Alicia Silverstone and friends perfectly send up privileged Beverly Hills of the era.

Dogtown and Z-Boys, 2002. This is a fun, high-spirited look at the glory times of skateboarding in the mid-1970s, when a daring group of Venice and Santa Monica kids took to using the empty swimming pools of the elite as their own private skate-parks.

LA Confidential, 1997. Perhaps the best of all the post-Chinatown LA noir films – a perfectly realized adaptation of James Ellroy's novel about brutal cops, victimized prostitutes, and scheming politicians in 1950s LA.

La La Land, 2016. Huge Oscar winner (six, including Best Picture) by Damien Chazelle, starring Ryan Gosling as a jazz pianist and Emma Stone as an aspiring actress; a homage to the musicals of Hollywood's Golden Age.

LA Story, 1991. Comedian Steve Martin's love-letter to LA is surprisingly relevant after all this time; jokes about Angelenos getting into their cars to travel just two blocks, or 25-year-old houses being considered ancient, still hold true.

Mulholland Drive, 2001. A frightening take on the city by director David Lynch, who uses nonlinear storytelling to present a tale of love, death, glamor, and doom.

Point Break, 1991. Pop favorite set in the surfer-dude world, with Keanu Reeves as a robbery-investigating FBI agent and Patrick Swayze as his rebel-surfer quarry.

Rebel Without a Cause, 1955. Fine, brash colors and widescreen composition in this troubled-youth movie, starring, of course, James Dean. A Hollywood classic with many memorable images, including Griffith Park Observatory as a shooting location.

Slums of Beverly Hills, 1998. Troubled teen Natasha Lyonne deals with growing pains in a less glamorous section of town, where a pill-popping cousin, manic uncle, weird neighbors, and her own expanding bust-line are but a few of her worries.

Straight Outta Compton, 2015. Warts-and-all depiction of the rise of Compton-based gangsta rap group N.W.A (named after their 1988 debut studio album), focusing on Eazy-E, Ice Cube, and Dr. Dre.

Sunset Boulevard, 1950. Award-winning movie about a screenwriter falling into the clutches of a long-faded silent-movie star. William Holden was near the beginning of his career, Gloria Swanson well past the end of hers.

Who Framed Roger Rabbit? 1988. Despite being a live-action/cartoon hybrid, this is a revealing movie about 1940s LA, where cartoon characters suffer abuse like everyone else and big corporations seek to destroy the Red Car transit system.

ABOUT THIS BOOK

This *Explore Guide* has been produced by the editors of Insight Guides, whose books have set the standard for visual travel guides since 1970. With top-quality photography and authoritative recommendations, these guidebooks bring you the very best routes and itineraries in the world's most exciting destinations.

BEST ROUTES

The routes in the book provide something to suit all budgets, tastes and trip lengths. As well as covering the destination's many classic attractions, the itineraries track lesser-known sights. The routes embrace a range of interests, so whether you are an art fan, a gourmet, a history buff or have kids to entertain, you will find an option to suit.

We recommend reading the whole of a route before setting out. This should help you to familiarise yourself with it and enable you to plan where to stop for refreshments – options are shown in the 'Food and Drink' box at the end of each tour.

For our pick of the tours by theme, consult Recommended Routes for… (see pages 6–7).

INTRODUCTION

The routes are set in context by this introductory section, giving an overview of the destination to set the scene, plus background information on food and drink, shopping and more, while a succinct history timeline highlights the key events over the centuries.

DIRECTORY

Also supporting the routes is a Directory chapter, with a clearly organised A–Z of practical information, our pick of where to stay while you are there and select restaurant listings; these eateries complement the more low-key cafés and restaurants that feature within the routes and are intended to offer a wider choice for evening dining. Also included here are some nightlife listings and our recommendations for books and films about the destination.

ABOUT THE AUTHORS

Stephen Keeling is an award-winning writer, journalist and editor. He has lived in various places around the world – from Latvia to Shanghai – before settling in New York in 2006. Stephen's knowledge of North America has been building ever since he started visiting Los Angeles in the early 1990s.

CONTACT THE EDITORS

We hope you find this Explore Guide useful, interesting and a pleasure to read. If you have any questions or feedback on the text, pictures or maps, please do let us know. If you have noticed any errors or outdated facts, or have suggestions for places to include on the routes, we would be delighted to hear from you. Please drop us an email at hello@insightguides.com. Thanks!

CREDITS

Explore Los Angeles
Editor: Helen Fanthorpe
Author: Stephen Keeling
Head of DTP and Pre-Press: Rebeka Davies
Picture Editor: Aude Vauconsant
Cartography: original cartography Carte
Photo credits: Alamy 10/11, 32, 62, 54, 55, 65, 74, 87, 105, 106/107, 110, 112, 113, 115, 118/119, 122/123; California Travel and Tourism Commission 6MC; Catherine Karnow/Apa Publications 28; Dale Robinette/Black Label Media/Kobal/REX/Shutterstock 137; Dan Bannister/Rough Guides 20; David Dunai/Apa Publications 16, 18/19, 48/49, 102MR, 127L; Getty Images 17, 24, 25, 40, 40/41, 43, 66/67, 69, 76/77, 78, 100, 101, 104, 108/109, 111, 114, 116, 117, 122, 123L; Glyn Genin/Apa Publications 26, 70; GRAMMY Museum 36; Henry Hargreaves/Nobu Restaurants 18, 102/103T; Hollywood Sign Trust 29; iStock 4ML, 4MC, 4MR, 4ML, 6TL, 6ML, 6BC, 7T, 7MR, 7M, 8/9T, 8ML, 8MR, 8MC, 8ML, 8MR, 11, 12T, 13, 14B, 14/15T, 21, 22, 23, 27, 30ML, 30MC, 30MR, 30ML, 30MC, 30MR, 30/31B, 33, 34, 35, 36/37, 37L, 38, 39, 42, 44, 45, 46/47, 50, 51, 56, 59, 60/61, 63, 64, 68, 72, 82/83, 89L, 88/89, 90, 92, 93L, 92/93, 98, 102ML, 102MR, 102ML, 120, 124/125, 126, 126/127, 128, 129, 130, 131L, 130/131, 132, 133, 134, 135; Shutterstock 1, 4MC, 7MR, 8MC, 12B, 19L, 41L, 52/53, 57L, 56/57, 58, 73L, 71, 72/73, 75, 79, 80, 81, 84/85, 86, 91, 94/95, 96, 97, 99, 102MC, 102MC, 121; Stahl House 88; StudioCanal/REX/Shutterstock 136; Susanne Kremer/4Corners Images 4/5T; Sushi Roku 4MR
Cover credits: Shutterstock (main&bottom)

Printed by CTPS – China

© 2018 Apa Digital (CH) AG and
Apa Publications (UK) Ltd
First Edition 2018

DISTRIBUTION

UK, Ireland and Europe
Apa Publications (UK) Ltd
sales@insightguides.com
United States and Canada
Ingram Publisher Services
ips@ingramcontent.com
Australia and New Zealand
Woodslane
info@woodslane.com.au
Southeast Asia
Apa Publications (Singapore) Pte
singaporeoffice@insightguides.com
Worldwide
Apa Publications (UK) Ltd
sales@insightguides.com

SPECIAL SALES, CONTENT LICENSING AND COPUBLISHING

Insight Guides can be purchased in bulk quantities at discounted prices. We can create special editions, personalised jackets and corporate imprints tailored to your needs.
sales@insightguides.com
www.insightguides.biz

INDEX